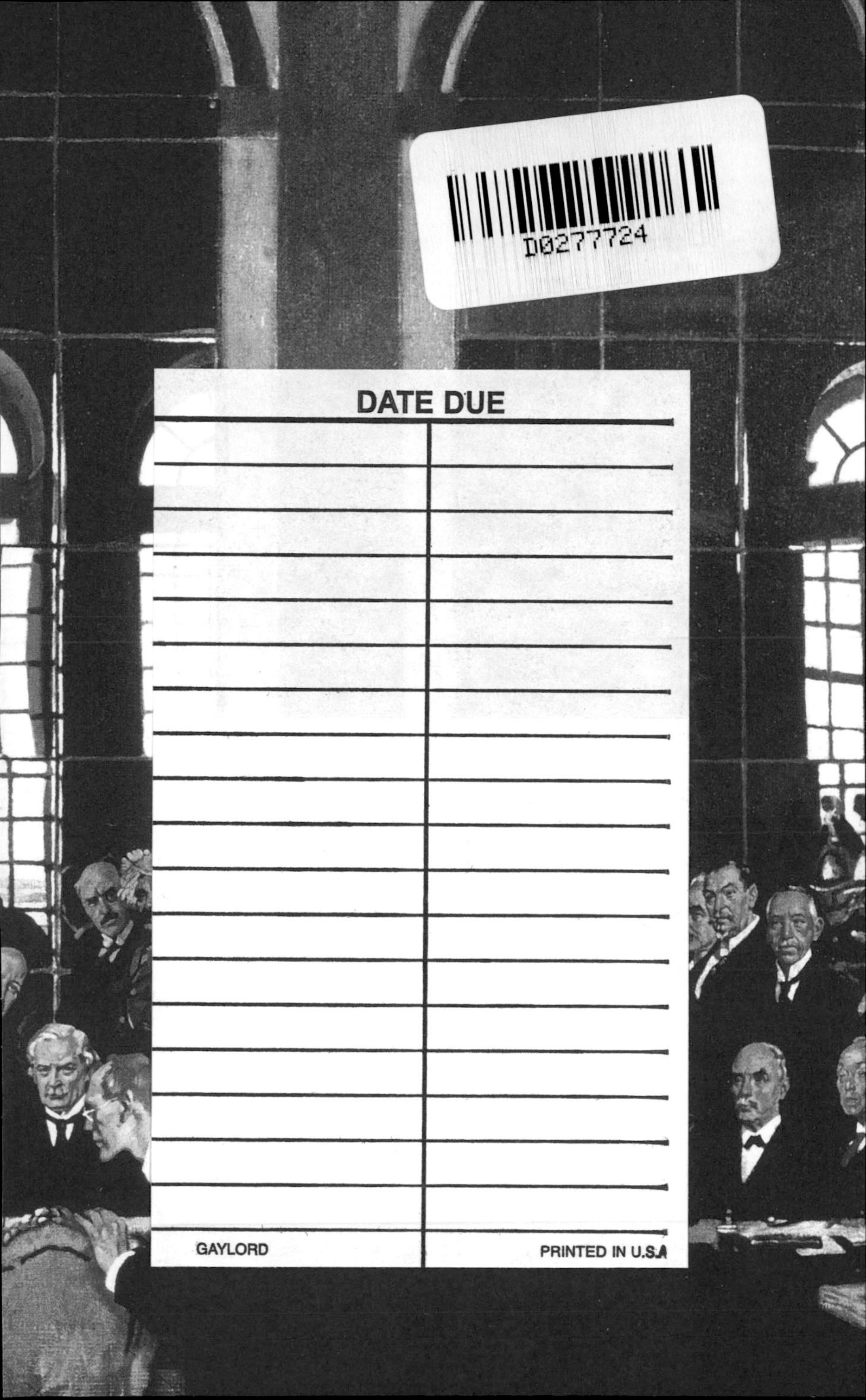

General Smuts

Makers
of the
Modern
World

General Smuts
South Africa
Antony Lentin

HH
HAUS HISTORIES

First published in Great Britain in 2010 by
Haus Publishing Ltd
70 Cadogan Place
London SW1X 9AH
www.hauspublishing.com

Copyright © Antony Lentin, 2010

The moral right of the author has been asserted

A CIP catalogue record for this book
is available from the British Library

ISBN 978-1-905791-82-8

Series design by Susan Buchanan
Typeset in Sabon by MacGuru Ltd
Printed in Dubai by Oriental Press
Map by Martin Lubikowski, ML Design, London

For S, F, A and T

History writes the word 'Reconciliation' over all her quarrels.
JAN CHRISTIAN SMUTS TO SIR ALFRED MILNER, 1905

Contents

Preface and Acknowledgements

'Choose well; your choice is
Brief and yet endless.'
JOHANN WOLFGANG VON GOETHE, 'PAST AND PRESENT',
QUOTED BY J C SMUTS, 12 JANUARY 1919[1]

'From 11 November 1918 to 28 June 1919 it was neither
chance nor the force of things that decided the outcome.
It was men, with their characters and their ideas. A
thousand provisions other than those adopted were
possible.'
JACQUES BAINVILLE, *THE POLITICAL CONSEQUENCES OF THE PEACE*, 1919[2]

Some years ago, Professor Gordon Martel berated historians
of the Paris Peace Conference, myself included, for harping
on a worn old tune and repeating, with variations, the familiar theme of the Conference as the tragic failure of the 20th
century.[3] Let me from the outset confess myself unrepentant.
I do not subscribe to the current scholarly consensus, which,
echoing that of the peacemakers of 1919, holds in effect that
they made the best of a bad job.[4] 'To know everything is to
understand everything', the proverb runs; but while recent
scholarship deepens our understanding of what happened at
Paris, it takes little account of the 'might-have-beens'.

For Jan Christian Smuts as for others at the Conference, the end of the First World War was a time pregnant with possibilities of what was then, for the first time, termed *a new world order*,[5] when, as Smuts put it, *things are fluid and plastic once more, and capable of receiving a new creative impression.*[6] This was no *mere superficial sentiment*,[7] but a conviction and a vision that had motivated and sustained many during the War. When the War ended and the Conference had not yet begun, Smuts reminded Woodrow Wilson that *this was the great opportunity in history.*[8]

The outcome was all the more chastening. Smuts, of all the Plenipotentiaries from first to last in my judgment the most principled, level-headed and far-sighted, argued that different decisions could and should have been taken, that a different treaty could have emerged, with happier results for mankind; that, in his words, *such a chance comes but once in a whole era of history – and we missed it.*[9] Nothing in a long life was to shake that conviction.

Shortly before his 80th birthday, Smuts remarked: *I belong to Antiquity.*[10] I felt this to be true in more than one sense and that Smuts was a universal man such as might have stepped from the pages of Plutarch. *I have touched life at so many points*,[11] he wrote – as warrior and commander in three wars, as scholar, jurist, scientist, philosopher (he read Spinoza at the Peace Conference) and as leader of his country and world statesman: withal a man of Spartan virtue admired for his courage and simplicity of life and character. Smuts's reputation today, however, is at a low ebb among historians who consider it their task to judge the past against current nostrums of 'equality' and 'diversity'.[12] Stretched on this procrustean bed, weighed in these anachronistic and unhistorical scales, Smuts inevitably emerges as a 'racist' and 'imperialist'.

Contemporaries saw him very differently. 'Even the great', wrote Alan Paton, 'thought that he was great.'[13]

Three thoughts in particular inspired this book. The first is a reflection of the diplomatist Harold Nicolson, whose own experience of Paris is distilled in classic form in his *Peacemaking 1919*. 'At any international Congress,' wrote Nicolson, 'it is the human element which determines both the development of negotiation and its issue.'[14] More than 30 years of thinking about the Conference has convinced me of this truth.

The second thought is a passing observation of Smuts himself. *When history is administered in biographical doses,* he remarked, *it becomes more than palatable.*[15] Much of Smuts's story can be told in his own words, for he was a prolific correspondent, never more so than at the Conference; and in his letters from Paris to a few chosen friends the historian disposes of a rich document of 'the human element', a chronicle of *one who saw and watched things from the inside*[16] and a register of his reactions to the Conference as it descended from its original high hopes to what he called *a tragedy of almost infinite dimensions.*[17]

The third thought to strike a responsive chord comes in a letter from Wilson to Smuts in 1921, two years after the momentous events in which both participated. 'I wish,' wrote Wilson, 'there might be someone to write discerningly and with knowledge of your own actions and influence at the Peace Conference, which were wholly admirable.'[18] I am not that 'someone'; but closer study of the evidence has reinforced my belief in the importance of Smuts's role which I have touched on in earlier studies of the Conference,[19] and leads me to hope that this brief account may be of interest in presenting another, perhaps less familiar aspect of what happened at Paris.

For giving me the opportunity to take up Wilson's challenge and to revisit yet again those haunted scenes now 90 years in the past where I and my colleagues have wandered so often in our mind's eye, and for his comments, my thanks are due to Professor Alan Sharp, who also generously furnished me with copies of primary sources. I must also thank Professor James Barber, Mrs Joy Brook, Professor A Hopkins, Dr R Hyam, Dr Susan Oosthuizen, Mrs Jenny Schotte, and Jaqueline Mitchell for her meticulous editing. Acknowledgments for material consulted or cited are due to the Bodleian Library, Oxford (Herbert Fisher Papers), the British Library (Lord Robert Cecil Papers), Cambridge University Library, Cambridge University Press and the Smuts Archive Trust (Smuts Papers), Churchill College, Cambridge (Hankey Papers), the House of Lords Record Office (Lloyd George Papers) and the National Archives, Kew (Foreign Office Papers).

Wolfson College, Cambridge

Prelude: 'I have fought and worked for a different peace'

Paris, Friday 30 May to Sunday 1 June 1919: a long weekend of glorious sunshine. But for much of it the British Empire Delegation to the Peace Conference is closeted indoors at a series of top-level crisis meetings convened and chaired by the Prime Minister, David Lloyd George. Upon the outcome of these meetings, Lloyd George rightly says, 'the peace of Europe and of the world might depend'.[1] The purpose of the meetings is to review the final terms of the peace treaty with Germany.

At the opening session on the Friday afternoon are present the British Empire Plenipotentiaries; that is, the Delegates duly empowered to sign the Treaty. They include the Prime Minister, the Foreign Secretary, the Colonial Secretary and others, and the accredited representatives of the Dominions of Canada, Australia and New Zealand, and, for the Union of South Africa, General Jan Christian Smuts, *a representative,* as he puts it, *of one of the smallest and least of the states at the Conference.*[2] Smuts speaks first and subjects the peace terms to detailed and powerful criticism. The meeting is adjourned until the Sunday to enable other leading members

PRESIDENT WILSON'S FOURTEEN POINTS, 8 JANUARY 1918

The program of the world's peace, therefore, is our program; and that program, the only possible program, as we see it, is this:

I. Open covenants of peace, openly arrived at, after which there shall be no private international understandings of any kind but diplomacy shall proceed always frankly and in the public view.

II. Absolute freedom of navigation upon the seas, outside territorial waters, alike in peace and in war, except as the seas may be closed in whole or in part by international action for the enforcement of international covenants.

III. The removal, so far as possible, of all economic barriers and the establishment of an equality of trade conditions among all the nations consenting to the peace and associating themselves for its maintenance.

IV. Adequate guarantees given and taken that national armaments will be reduced to the lowest point consistent with domestic safety.

V. A free, open-minded, and absolutely impartial adjustment of all colonial claims, based upon a strict observance of the principle that in determining all such questions of sovereignty the interests of the populations concerned must have equal weight with the equitable claims of the government whose title is to be determined.

VI. The evacuation of all Russian territory and such a settlement of all questions affecting Russia as will secure the best and freest cooperation of the other nations of the world in obtaining for her an unhampered and unembarrassed opportunity for the independent determination of her own political development and national policy and assure her of a sincere welcome into the society of free nations under institutions of her own choosing; and, more than a welcome, assistance also of every kind that she may need and may herself desire. The treatment accorded Russia by her sister nations in the months to come will be the acid test of their good will, of their comprehension of her needs as distinguished from their own interests, and of their intelligent and unselfish sympathy.

VII. Belgium, the whole world will agree, must be evacuated and restored, without any attempt to limit the sovereignty which she enjoys in common with all other free nations. No other single act will serve as this will serve to restore confidence among the nations in the laws which they have themselves set and determined for the government of their relations with one another. Without this healing act the whole structure and validity of international law is forever impaired.

VIII. All French territory should be freed and the invaded portions restored, and the wrong done to France by Prussia in 1871 in the matter of Alsace-Lorraine, which has unsettled the peace of the world for nearly fifty years, should be righted, in order that peace may once more be made secure in the interest of all.

IX. A readjustment of the frontiers of Italy should be effected along clearly recognizable lines of nationality.

X. The peoples of Austria-Hungary, whose place among the nations we wish to see safeguarded and assured, should be accorded the freest opportunity to autonomous development.

XI. Rumania, Serbia, and Montenegro should be evacuated; occupied territories restored; Serbia accorded free and secure access to the sea; and the relations of the several Balkan states to one another determined by friendly counsel along historically established lines of allegiance and nationality; and international guarantees of the political and economic independence and territorial integrity of the several Balkan states should be entered into.

XII. The Turkish portion of the present Ottoman Empire should be assured a secure sovereignty, but the other nationalities which are now under Turkish rule should be assured an undoubted security of life and an absolutely unmolested opportunity of autonomous development, and the Dardanelles should be permanently opened as a free passage to the ships and commerce of all nations under international guarantees.

XIII. An independent Polish state should be erected which should include the territories inhabited by indisputably Polish populations, which should be assured a free and secure access to the sea, and whose political and economic independence and territorial integrity should be guaranteed by international covenant.

XIV. A general association of nations must be formed under specific covenants for the purpose of affording mutual guarantees of political independence and territorial integrity to great and small states alike.

of the British Government, specially summoned from London, to add their counsels at an enlarged extraordinary meeting. The Saturday, while these Ministers cross to France, is a free day. Smuts relaxes in the forest of Saint Germain-en-Laye, but with feelings of foreboding.

When the Plenary Session opens on the Sunday, Smuts again denounces the Treaty as *an impossible document*.[3] He reminds his colleagues of what he calls the *Wilson Peace* proclaimed in President Wilson's Fourteen Points speech and related speeches of 1918. At the Armistice of November 1918 the Allies had offered, and Germany had accepted, a ceasefire on the promise of a peace based on the Points, Principles and Particulars enunciated by the President in those speeches. Those declarations are no mere expression of pious aspirations; they are *bedrock,* says Smuts: the legal foundation of a solemn international agreement. He contrasts them with what he calls the *scrap of paper*[4] in front of them. (In 1814 Germany invaded Belgium in violation of a treaty of 1839 guaranteeing Belgium's neutrality, to which Prussia was a signatory. The German Chancellor, Bethmann-Hollweg, described the treaty as 'a scrap of paper'.) The peace of 1919, says Smuts, is not a *Wilson peace* at all but *a bad peace,* unjust, impractical and containing *the*

> I view it as a thoroughly bad peace – impolitic and impracticable in the case of Germany, absolutely ludicrous in the case of German Austria. Indeed I have not been able to read the comments of the Austrian delegates on our draft terms without deep emotion. I have fought this Peace from the inside with all my power, and have no doubt been able in the end to secure some small openings of hope for the future.
>
> J C SMUTS TO C P SCOTT, EDITOR OF THE *MANCHESTER GUARDIAN*, 26 JUNE 1919[10]

roots of war.[5] He will not vote for it and he doubts whether he can sign it. Three weeks later, despite some partial amendments which he describes as *paltry,*[6] he confirms to a friend, *I am not going to sign it on any account.*[7] But five days later, on 28 June 1919, at the final ceremony in the Hall of Mirrors, his mind *numbed* and with a heart *dry with sorrow and shame*[8] he signs the Treaty of Versailles. *I have failed,* he confesses, *at the most critical point in human history.*[9] Significantly his portrait is absent from Sir William Orpen's famous tableau of the ceremony.

At the core of this book is an account of Smuts at the Peace Conference, for him, as he told his biographer, the 'unhappiest time of his life'.[11] *I have fought and worked for a different peace,* he wrote to his wife, *a peace of reconciliation and recovery among the nations.*[12] To C P Scott, editor of the *Manchester Guardian* – the same admission of defeat: *I have fought this Peace from the inside with all my power.*[13] He had lost the fight. His six months at the Conference profoundly affected him. *Paris showed me the crack in life itself,* he said. *It broke me. It changed me.*[14]

Jan Christian Smuts in 1917. 'What a man! His sense of values takes one away from Paris and this greedy turmoil', wrote Harold Nicolson on Smuts in his diary for 11 April 1919.

I

The Life and the Land

1

Smuts – Scholar, Statesman, Soldier: 1870–1914

South Africa first impinged on European history in 1488, when the Portuguese explorer Bartholomew Diaz rounded what was later named the Cape of Good Hope. European settlement dates from 1652, when the Dutchman Jan Van Riebeeck established a victualling station there for the Dutch East India Company. The 17th and 18th centuries saw the gradual expansion of this Dutch possession until the start of Britain's wars with Revolutionary and Napoleonic France, when Britain seized Cape Town as a staging post on the route to India. After briefly ceding the Cape Colony to Holland (then the Batavian Republic, a French satellite) under the Peace of Amiens in 1803, Britain annexed it in 1806 when Napoleon annexed Holland to the French Empire.

The Boers (the word means 'farmers') were mainly of Dutch Calvinist descent, who intermarried with French Huguenots and Germans. Many of them disliked British rule, not least because of Britain's abolition of slavery throughout the Empire in 1833. Not for another two centuries would these Calvinists concede equality in any sense to the black men who served them as hewers of wood and drawers of water, and there was resentment among the Boers at British pressure on their outlook and way of life. In 1836 there began the Great Trek, when Boers from the frontiers of the Cape Colony struck out north and east with their ox-wagons and their cattle in search of freedom from British rule. Anticipating their penetration to the Indian Ocean, Britain annexed Natal in 1843. The Boer pioneers, the *Voortrekkers*, established their independence beyond the Rivers Vaal and Orange, driving the native peoples from their land in what eventually became the Boer Republics of the Transvaal and Transoranje (later the Orange Free State). From the first, the Boer Republics were land-locked, hemmed into the interior by piecemeal British annexation of adjacent territories. They were also inward-looking and exclusive. The Transvaal Constitution laid down that there should be 'no equality between coloured people and the white inhabitants, either in Church or State'.[1]

Antagonism between the British and Boers intensified with the discovery of diamonds on the Orange River in 1867. Findings of still richer deposits three years later at Kimberley in Griqualand West on the border of the two Boer Republics led to Britain's annexation of that territory in 1877. An attempt to seize the Transvaal itself ended disastrously for Britain in the First Boer War (1880–1881), when Boer guerrillas wiped out a British force at Majuba Hill. When gold was also discovered in the Transvaal on the Witwatersrand around Johannesburg in 1883, an influx of prospectors and adventurers began. The economy of South Africa was transformed, the Transvaal producing one-third of the world's annual gold supply and more than half its diamonds. Among the magnates with a commanding interest in both commodities was Cecil Rhodes, founder of the De Beers Diamond

Company and the Consolidated Goldfields of South Africa. As non-Boer immigrants, known as *Uitlanders* (foreigners), mainly British, many from Cape Colony and Natal, continued to pour into the Transvaal in their thousands, the Boers felt their devout, pastoral and patriarchal way of life to be under threat. 'They have grown fat on my land,' complained the President of the Transvaal, the dour and autocratic Paul Kruger, who had come north with the *Voortrekkers* as a boy of 10. 'They are richer than our own people.'[2] What more, he asked indignantly, did the *Uitlanders* want? What they wanted, as the main taxpayers in the Transvaal, was political representation; but Kruger doggedly tightened existing restrictions on the franchise and told them to leave if they did not like it. Meanwhile Britain was entering a more aggressive phase of expansionist imperialism and the cause of the *Uitlanders* offered a ready-made excuse for intervention.

The first Smuts came to Cape Town from Holland as a settler in 1692. His descendant, Jan Christian Smuts, was born a British subject on 24 May 1870 in his father's modest farmhouse at Bovenplaats, near the Boer hamlet of Riebeeck West in the rich, wheat-growing Malmesbury district to the west of the Cape Colony, 45 miles from Cape Town. The Smuts's had farmed here for four generations. Jan's father, Jacobus Abraham Smuts, was a pillar of the Dutch Reformed Church and an inconspicuous member of the Colonial Parliament at Cape Town. His eldest son, Michiel, was intended for the ministry, and it was customary for the younger son not to be sent to school; so Jan, who, it was planned, would one day take over the farm, was brought up by his mother. His childhood was simple and frugal. Until he was 12, he tended the sheep and cattle on the farm. Here, amid meadows, veld and mountains, in the shadow of the Kasteel mountain and the

Great Winterhoek range beyond, he developed *a passion for nature*,[3] a Wordsworthian sense of intimate communion with the natural world. *Those hills of my beginnings always have a great effect on me*,[4] he wrote.

On Michiel's sudden death from typhoid, it was decided that Jan should take his place and be educated with a view to entering the church. So at the age of 12 he first attended the village school at Riebeeck West. Afrikaans was his mother tongue. At school he heard English virtually for the first time. He immediately revealed a passion, wholly unexpected, for learning, and matching powers of absorption. He took the higher school examination within four years instead of the usual 11 and entered Victoria College (later Stellenbosch University) in 1886 at the age of 16.

Smuts always spoke with the distinctive Malmesbury burr, a guttural pronunciation of the letter 'r'. The accent, typical of the Western Cape, while not harsh, sounds to some more German than the accent of the northern Afrikaner. To one Englishman his accent was 'rather like that of a Welshman'.[5] Settling down to his studies at Stellenbosch, Smuts found that he was required to take Greek. During the holidays he locked himself in his room and, with tremendous application and endowed with a photographic memory, mastered a Greek grammar and a book of Attic prose in a week and came top in the Greek matriculation examination. He also became proficient in Netherlands Dutch and German. But he was always at his best in English.

In his years at Stellenbosch, Smuts, 5 feet 10 inches tall, fair-skinned and blond, was of slender build, a 'pallid, slight, delicate-looking man',[6] reserved, fastidious, serious-minded and solitary, a devotee of the library who shunned the sports field, a regular attender at the Dutch Reformed Church, an occasional Sunday-school teacher[7] and, as he admitted, something of a prig. He held himself aloof from his fellow students, with one exception: the pretty and highly gifted Sybella Krige – known as Isie – whom he fell in love with at the age of 17 and would marry 10 years later. The two found companionship in books, poetry (especially Goethe and Shelley) and music. They sang German *Lieder* together with Isie at the piano. Isie was more outgoing than Jan and it was she, he wrote, who *recalled me from my intellectual isolation and made me return to my fellows.*[8]

In 1891, Smuts gained a double first in the joint literature and science degree at Stellenbosch. He won a scholarship to read law at Cambridge, and made the first of many journeys to England, suffering, as he always did, agonies of seasickness. At Cambridge, he was elected a Scholar of Christ's College, but money was short and he led an austere life, hardworking and lonely. A rare friend was a reclusive middle-aged don named John Wolstenholme. Some fellow students from South Africa once took him to London to see the Boat Race, but he gave them the slip and spent the day in the library of the Middle Temple. Smuts read widely, deeply and retentively, as he was to do all his life, in classical, biblical and modern literature, science and philosophy. *At Cambridge*, he wrote, *I read much, walked much and thought much, and when I left the University I had probably drunk as deeply of the well of knowledge as most.*[9] He proved to be one of Cambridge's most outstanding law students. His tutor, the great legal scholar Frederick Maitland, considered him the best he ever taught. He sat both parts of the Law Tripos simultaneously, an achievement without precedent, headed the list of candidates with a double first and won prizes in jurisprudence and Roman law. He was also developing, independently, the holistic philosophy which he was later to make his own; and while still an undergraduate he wrote a book, unpublished in his lifetime, entitled *Walt Whitman: A Study in the Evolution of Personality*,[10] which contained the germ of holism. Whitman's poetry liberated him from an outlook that had been, he said, *severely puritanical*.[11]

In 1894 he paid a brief visit to Strasbourg, then in Germany, to study literature and philosophy. Returning to England, he read for the Bar as a student of the Middle Temple, and after call practiced briefly as a barrister. Turning down a law fellowship at Christ's – Maitland said he had the makings of a great scholar of Roman law – he returned to South Africa in 1895 to set up in practice at Cape Town. He failed initially to make his mark in the law, but threw himself into politics and supported himself with journalism. He joined the Afrikaner Bond Party of Jan Hendrik Hofmeyr, which, while representing Boer interests, shared the aspirations of the Cape Dutch and Cape English for a common South African nationhood, a cause also championed by the Prime Minister of the Cape Colony, Cecil Rhodes.

Smuts was an enthusiastic supporter of Rhodes. He believed fervently in a partnership between *the two Teutonic peoples*, Dutch-speaking and English-speaking, together comprising some half-million whites *at the southern corner of a vast continent peopled*, as he put it, *by over 100 million barbarians*.[12] This view of the majority population, though tempered by a paternalistic and kindly attitude to individual blacks, remained his lifelong conviction. Rhodes was a Promethean figure, carried away by his imperialist vision of British rule from Cape Town to Cairo, and his reckless impatience brought disaster. His involvement in the Jameson Raid into the Transvaal in December 1895, *that fatal and*

THE JAMESON RAID

The Transvaalers, a small, devout and pastoral people, found their way of life and independence threatened by the influx of prospectors, mainly British expatriates, known as *Uitlanders* (foreigners). 30,000 Boer voters lived in the Transvaal with 60,000 *Uitlanders,* whose enfranchisement was tightly restricted. The *Uitlanders'* grievances were exploited with a view to overthrowing the government of President Kruger by a raid on Johannesburg and a local uprising of *Uitlanders* in December 1895. The raid was planned by Cecil Rhodes, Prime Minister of the Cape Colony, and mounted by Leander Starr Jameson (himself later also Prime Minister of the Cape Colony). The raid brought Anglo-Boer relations to a dangerous low. The Transvaal, enriched by the revenues from the goldmines, began importing arms, concluded an alliance with the Orange Free State in 1897 and intrigued for Germany's support, while the British Colonial Secretary, Joseph Chamberlain, welcomed the escalation of tension as an opportunity to annex the Boer Republics. Smuts wrote later that *the Jameson raid was the real declaration of war*[13] leading to the Second Boer War, 1899–1902.

perfidious venture,[14] revealed to Smuts that his trust in Rhodes, now discredited and ousted from the Premiership, had been misplaced; and that Rhodes's ambition, in which the British Colonial Secretary, Joseph Chamberlain, was also implicated, was for nothing less than a British takeover of the Boer Republics.

In 1896, deceived in Rhodes and utterly disenchanted, Smuts left the Cape Colony for the Transvaal, renouncing his British citizenship to throw in his lot with his own people. Setting up as a lawyer in Johannesburg, he married his sweetheart, Isie Krige, in 1897. Twins were born to them prematurely in 1898 but died shortly after. Smuts's legal expertise attracted the attention of the 74-year-old Kruger, who in 1898 appointed him, aged only 28, as *Staats Procureur* or State Attorney, responsible for law and order in the Transvaal and legal adviser to the government. When Kruger summarily dismissed his Chief Justice, an action widely denounced as unconstitutional, Smuts took the opposite view and forcefully defended Kruger's action. A deep mutual regard sprang up between these two very different men. Their relations, Smuts recalled, were *like those of father and son*.[15] Smuts, for all his Cambridge learning, admired Kruger's rugged integrity, while Kruger perceived in the bright young lawyer an 'iron will'[16] and predicted he would play a great part in the history of South Africa. Smuts now moved to the capital, Pretoria, and soon had a leading voice in the counsels of the Transvaal as it faced growing tension with the *Uitlanders*.

He strove conscientiously to address the *Uitlanders'* legitimate grievances while defending the sovereignty of the Republic from British pressure. He urged franchise reform on Kruger and believed he had come close to agreement with Joseph Chamberlain. *God alone knows*, he wrote, *how deeply I wished, how hard I worked that peace might be maintained*.[17] Kruger, however, was convinced, and rightly so, that the cause of the *Uitlanders* was a pretext for annexation. At a final meeting with the British at Bloemfontein in August 1899 to see whether compromise was possible, Smuts accompanied Kruger as his adviser. 'It's our country that you want,'[18] Kruger told Sir Alfred Milner, Governor-General of the Cape and High Commissioner for South Africa. Milner, like Rhodes an ardent imperialist, who treated Smuts with marked hostility, was indeed bent on forcing the issue in Britain's favour. In October Kruger sought to pre-empt Milner while British troops in South Africa were still few. He issued an ultimatum, drafted by Smuts, demanding their withdrawal. This led immediately to the Second Boer War, known to the Boers as the Second War of Liberation.

The Second Boer War

Having done his utmost to avoid war, Smuts was now totally committed to defending the independence of his adoptive country. In all but name he was First Minister of the Transvaal and, though without military experience, he showed a remarkable grasp both of strategy and of the need to husband and deploy the resources at his disposal. He wrote an impassioned Afrikaner manifesto, *A Century of Wrong*, in which he called on Boers from across South Africa to unite against the British *as Leonidas with his 300 at Thermopylae in the face of the vast hordes of Xerxes.*[19] The Orange Free State threw in its lot with the Transvaal and Smuts argued that the two Republics should invade Natal and the Cape Province, whose Afrikaner citizens were in sympathy with their fellow Boers, to forestall a British build-up of forces.

Smuts's advice was rejected. Hopes of German intervention came to nothing, and despite successful early offensives by the Boers, culminating in December 1899 in 'Black Week', when the British suffered three crushing reverses in succession, the veteran Afrikaner generals of the First Boer War proved, as Smuts complained, *hopelessly incompetent*,[20] wasting their advantages through over-caution and delay. British troops, shipped out to South Africa in their thousands under Lord Roberts and Lord Kitchener, quickly overran the Boer Republics. Pretoria fell to Roberts in June 1900. Kruger fled abroad, and Britain proclaimed the annexation of the Transvaal and Orange Free State as Crown Colonies. In Britain there was jubilation, but it was premature, for the war was far from over. It now entered its longest and most critical phase.

Smuts, resourceful and determined, now began a new chapter in his life. For the next two years, a rebel in British eyes, he became what would now be called a 'freedom fighter'.

Though nominally only State Attorney, he found himself in sole charge of the government of the collapsing Transvaal. Bidding farewell to Isie and a newly born son (who died a few months later), he escaped from Pretoria, first making sure of removing the country's stock of ammunition and extracting its gold reserves at gunpoint from the National Bank, secreting them out of the country by special train just before the town fell to the British and *while shells were bursting all around the station*.[21] These reserves helped to maintain Boer resistance for the rest of the war.

Smuts took charge of one of the commando units into which the 60,000-strong Boer forces divided. These units consisted of bodies of horsemen, each a few hundred strong, operating independently. These slouch-hatted sharp-shooters ranged far and wide across *the illimitable veld*,[22] living off the land and aided by local farmers. They waged guerrilla war as opportunity arose, with spectacular success. The individual units, virtually bands of freebooters, were led by Generals Christian de Wet, James Barry Hertzog (later Smuts's political rival), Koos de La Rey and Smuts himself, also now a general, under the overall command of General Louis Botha. After hard-fought attempts to beat the British in the Magaliesberg Mountains north of Pretoria and in the Western Transvaal, where Smuts hoped to retake Johannesburg, the generals decided in June 1901 on a different strategy. While Botha set off eastward for Natal, Smuts, in accordance with his original plan, headed south for the Cape.

Nothing in his career hitherto hinted at what followed, as he led his commandos in an epic series of stratagems of his devising, undergoing hair-breadth escapes that have become the stuff of legend. This heroic saga stands comparison with Xenophon's *Anabasis* ('the march up-country' through Asia

Minor of 10,000 Greeks seeking to regain their homeland, 401–399 BC), a copy of which Smuts found in an abandoned farmhouse. Smuts's own exploits were immortalized in *Commando* (1929) by the young Deneys Reitz, who fought under him.

Evading British detachments sent to intercept him, Smuts crossed the Orange River in September 1901, leading a body of 350 picked men into the Cape Colony. On this eight-month long odyssey across 2,000 miles of vast and varied terrain, gathering volunteers along the way, he journeyed south to within sight of Port Elizabeth and westward to his old home near Cape Town, then struck up through Bushman territory to the far north, close to German South-West Africa. He coolly devised and boldly launched dozens of hit-and-run raids against detachments of a British force totalling 35,000, from whom he took guns, ammunition, horses, provisions and even boots and uniforms, without which, he said, his men would *have been compelled to go naked*.[23] The British proclaimed that any Boer found in British uniform would be shot, and they offered a £1,000 reward for Smuts's capture, dead or alive. They occupied his house at Pretoria and ransacked his library. They took Isie to Natal and kept her under surveillance for 18 months.

The commandos lived in constant peril and privation, subject to hunger and exhaustion in the pelting rain and bitter cold of the winter of 1901. As a young man Smuts had been thought delicate. 'Drink beer, my boy,' his doctor at Cambridge had advised, 'It will do you good.'[24] Now, amid gruelling marches and bloody skirmishes on the open veld and high mountain ranges, he showed himself hardy, seasoned, bold and resourceful. He showed amazing endurance and the capacity to withstand fatigue, pitting himself day after day against the elements and the constant hazard of injury or death, harried by day by the British, at night sharing a tattered blanket with a comrade, for they slept in twos for warmth. On one occasion, however, he and his men were taken violently ill when a fruit of appetizing appearance which they hungrily devoured turned out to be poisonous, an episode he often related with amusement. In the most adverse circumstances Smuts remained cheerful, undaunted and resolved. In a rare letter to Isie, he was positively exultant: *I have never been in better health or spirits in my life*, he wrote. *Military life agrees wonderfully with me.*[25]

Smuts led from the front. He always reconnoitred personally to assess a situation for himself. He led a charmed life, braving ambush, pursuit and enemy fire. In one encounter his horse was shot from under him, his escorts were killed and he *alone escaped in miraculous fashion.*[26] On two occasions he was almost hit by exploding shells. Had he been killed, wrote Deneys Reitz, 'the expedition to the Cape would have come to a speedy end', for no there was no other leader with his 'personality or the influence over men ... to save us from going to pieces.'[27] Smuts himself was affected more *by the shame of capture than by the fear of being killed.*[28] *I have had numerous escapes in this war*, he wrote, *for which I am grateful*, adding fatalistically: *but each person has his time.*[29] He showed the same physical and moral courage throughout his life, almost as if he dared destiny to do its worst.

Whenever he could snatch a moment, he read. Apart from Xenophon, he packed in his saddlebag at various times a Cicero, an English Bible, a volume of Schiller and Immanuel Kant's *Critique of Pure Reason*, books mostly picked up along the way. *One of the pleasures of capturing an English convoy*, he recalled, *was the number of English books found among the officers' kit.*[30] Always with him was a Greek New Testament, for this lone philosopher continually pondered the ultimate things, whether on the march or bivouacked at night *under the open African sky*, where *some of the deepest emotional experiences of my life have come to me.*[31] His courage, flair and martial qualities won the devotion of his men, the respect of Afrikaners generally and the admiration of the British, who regarded Smuts and Botha as the finest of the Boer generals and Smuts as the most chivalrous to his captives. He wasted no sympathy, however, on traitors. A renegade Boer spy cost the lives of 17 of Smuts's men. Smuts had him court-martialed. His guilt was undisputed. *Take him out and shoot him,*[32] Smuts ordered. Always decisive, once he had made up his mind, he never fretted or repined.

In December 1901, his unit reached the Atlantic. Many of his men had never seen the sea before; they shed their clothes and galloped their horses headlong into the surf. But as for the war, the odds were hopeless. Despite the striking success of their hit-and-run tactics, the commandos could not hope to overcome the relentless pursuit of the endless British columns. General Kitchener, now Commander-in-Chief, disposed over 400,000 men. Yet the decisive factor was not military but civilian: the harsh counter-measures which Kitchener adopted to contain and close in on the civilians and destroy the commandos' supply-routes.

> ... The groans of the dying and the blanched set faces of the dead... were enough to drive away all unwholesome feelings of exultation, and to remind one of the grim reality that war is. And even though these were the faces and the sufferings of our enemy, one had... a deeper sense of the common humanity which knows no racial distinctions.
>
> **J C SMUTS ON THE BOER WAR**[33]

Kitchener wore down the Afrikaners and their families, rounding them up in great sweeps and a relentless scorched-earth strategy in which their land was laid waste, their cattle slaughtered and their farmsteads burned to the ground.

The women and children were herded into concentration camps, a term having then its literal meaning, but where mortality from starvation and disease was dire, leaving a dark blot on Britain's reputation and a lasting legacy of bitterness in the hearts of the Boers. The scandal of the camps was brought to public attention in Britain by the radical campaigner Emily Hobhouse, who went to South Africa to see them for herself and to bring practical aid to the sufferers. She gave evidence of what she had seen to the leader of the Liberal opposition, Sir Henry Campbell-Bannerman, who denounced the Government for employing 'methods of barbarism'.[34] After the war Emily Hobhouse became a friend of Smuts, and impressed on him and on the Liberal leaders in Britain his potential as a spokesman of Boer opinion – 'to be the tongue of your people'[35].

Defeat

For the game was up. In April 1902, when Kitchener offered a truce and peace talks at Vereeniging, the Boer generals accepted. The generals and delegates from across the country came to Vereeniging, grim, gaunt, ragged and worn from their campaigning. They first debated hard amongst themselves. Some were broken men; others were determined to fight on. The argument went back and forth between what the rival sides called the 'bitter-enders' and the 'hands-uppers'. Then Smuts spoke. *I learnt to bow my head to the inevitable*,[36] he recalled. To his comrades-in-arms in their anguish he spoke words of truth and courage and rallied them to face facts. It was true that they were unbeaten. From a *military point of view*, he agreed, *we can still go on with the struggle*. It was also true that *we decided to stand to the bitter end. Let us now*, he said, *like men, admit that the end has come*.[37] Altogether, 4,000 Boer fighters had been killed in the war as against 22,000 British troops; but 28,000 Boer women and children, more than one-tenth of the population of the Boer Republics, had perished in the camps. At a conference with Milner and Kitchener, Generals Smuts, Botha, de Wet, de la Rey, and Hertzog, accepted terms of settlement, and the Peace of Vereeniging was signed on 31 May 1902. There was no scope for negotiation. Milner was inflexible and demanded capitulation. The Republics remained annexed and the whole of South Africa came under British rule.

> **The tragedy is over. The curtain falls over the Boers as British subjects and the plucky little republics are no more … Let us do our best to bind up the old wounds, to forgive and forget and to make the future happier than the past has been.**
>
> J C SMUTS, 1 JUNE 1902, THE DAY AFTER THE SIGNING OF THE ANGLO–BOER TREATY OF VEREENIGING[38]

The peace had to be accomplished,[39] Smuts recalled, when he advised that the Republics must be sacrificed and incorporation into the Empire accepted. Yet Kitchener had called him aside at Vereeniging and privately suggested the possibility of more generous terms in the likely event of the return of a Liberal government in England. From his Cambridge days, Smuts had memories of the tradition of *that other England, the England of John Bright*,[40] and he was cheered by the opposition to the Boer War of a small but articulate minority of Liberal politicians, including Campbell-Bannerman and Lloyd George.

Meanwhile, tried and hardened by war and with a formidable reputation for leadership, the 32-year-old Smuts needed to regain his livelihood. No longer State Attorney of an independent Republic, he strove to re-establish himself as a junior barrister at the Pretoria Bar. Success at last came his way and he invested his earnings in land. *Land does not run away,*[41] he used to say. Two daughters were born to Isie by the end of 1904, followed during the next decade by another two girls and two boys. The Smuts's also had an adopted daughter, for Smuts had a unique rapport with small children, in whose company he joyfully unwound. The infants he dandled in his arms were invariably fascinated by the short beard which he now sported.

Immediate political prospects for the Boers were unpropitious, and Smuts, suffering a *mood of ennui,*[42] a natural reaction after his exertions in the war, was depressed and embittered by the humiliation of national defeat and subjugation. Milner continued to lord it as High Commissioner for South Africa, *this blessed satrapy,*[43] as Smuts called it. Now a Viscount and Governor of the Transvaal Colony and (as it was renamed) Orange River Colony, Milner directed South Africa's post-war reconstruction with a vigorous and generous but autocratic proconsular hand and a team of young Englishmen known as his 'kindergarten'. Smuts compared Milner to the Bey of Tunis and refused his offer of a nominated place in the Transvaal legislative council. Smuts adopted an attitude of sullen stoicism, his philosophy: to *water my orange trees and read Kant's Critique of Pure Reason.*[44]

'The greatest experience of my life'

Increasingly, however, Smuts was coming under the spell of Botha. It was Botha, the elder by eight years, who first had the vision and courage to aspire to work for a new South Africa, making a conscious resolve to draw a line under the lost war and the feuds and resentments of the past. Smuts at first stood apart, in self-conscious solidarity with his fellow-Afrikaners, proud and unbending under *the bondage imposed upon them at Vereeniging*;[45] but he was won over to Botha's larger view by the *sheer humanity and sympathy*[46] of the man. Moved by Botha's magnanimity and inspired by his example – *I have never*, he recalled, *in any other man seen such a fine power of sympathy*[47] – he too came to feel cleansed and humanised *in the fires of adversity*,[48] able to put bitterness behind him and to embrace a new creative vision of the future. An irrepressible and infectious optimism came to his aid. *Alles sal reg kom*[49] – 'everything will come right'– a phrase often on his lips, expressed his new outlook. Henceforth Smuts and Botha worked together in unbroken harmony – *as close together as it is ever given to men to come*.[50] They became the recognized political leaders in the Transvaal. Together with Koos de la Rey, they founded in 1904 a political movement known as Vereeniging Het Volk (People's Union) or simply Het Volk, dedicated to self-government within the Empire and reconciliation between Boer and Briton. (Hertzog founded a similar movement in the Orange River Colony.) Smuts was active in rallying Afrikaner opposition to Milner's policies on education and language which favoured the British and to his deeply unpopular decision to import 50,000 Chinese labourers to make up a shortage of workers in the gold mines.

Milner's tenure came to an end in 1905. For all their differences, Smuts sent him a valedictory letter in a new and friendlier spirit. *History writes the word 'Reconciliation' over all her quarrels*,[51] he wrote to his old enemy. In the same year the Conservative government in Britain also ran its course. A general election took place in December, and Botha sent Smuts to London as the representative of Het Volk to put the case for the Transvaal to the leaders of the Liberal Party. He came in good faith and with high hopes. *I love England*, he told reporters on his arrival. *I was educated here.*[52]

It was on this visit that Smuts underwent a further experience that fed his newfound optimism and profoundly shaped his life and outlook. He renewed his acquaintance with a Quaker family, the Clarks, shoe manufacturers of Street in Somerset, and with the Clark sisters, Alice and Margaret in particular. On their mother's side, Alice and Margaret were granddaughters of the Victorian Quaker and radical pacifist John Bright, and so were literally representative of *the England of John Bright*.[53] The Clarks opposed the Boer War and Margaret had gone out to South Africa with Emily Hobhouse to assist in the work of rehabilitation. It was there that she first met Smuts. The two sailed on the same ship when Smuts came to England in 1905, and immediately on his arrival he went to visit the family in Street.

This visit inspired his liking for the simple Quaker mode of worship and for the radical idealism of the Clarks. His religious leanings had broadened far beyond the Dutch Calvinism of his youth and he had long ceased to be a conventional churchgoer; but he gladly joined in the silent worship in the Friends' Meeting House. He shared the Quaker belief in the promptings of conscience and the inner light, and in the course of many country walks with the Clarks he felt confirmed in his sense of the divine in nature which he had first experienced in boyhood amid the mountains and veld around Riebeeck West. Margaret became his lifelong confidante, his soul-mate and *best friend on earth*.[54] When she married Arthur Gillett in 1909 and moved to Oxford, the Gilletts' house at 102 Banbury Road became Smuts's second home in England.

From Street Smuts went to London to canvas the Liberal leaders for responsible government in the Boer colonies. Those he approached first were sympathetic but sceptical. Then came his interview with Campbell-Bannerman. Smuts's case was simple: *Do you want friends or enemies?* he asked. The Boers had *proved what quality their friendship* could mean. To make enemies of them could mean *another Ireland on your hands.* Campbell-Bannerman, Smuts recalled, *said nothing to me, but yet… my intuition told me that the thing had been done.*[55] At any rate, in February 1906 when the Liberals returned to office with a landslide majority, one of their first actions was to restore self-government to the Transvaal and Orange Free State as Provinces of British South Africa.

The Prime Minister's legendary conversion was an episode to which Smuts returned time and again in the course of his life. It would be impossible to exaggerate its impact on him. His version of it may well be overdrawn. Campbell-Bannerman, by Smuts's own account *a cautious Scot,*[56] may have concealed from him that he had already made up his mind. The fact remains that had he not wholeheartedly championed the new policy, it would not have come into being. The day after Smuts's interview, Campbell-Bannerman made to his Cabinet what Lloyd George called 'the most dramatic, the most important ten-minute's speech ever delivered in our time',[57] and the Cabinet approved his momentous decision. It was bitterly opposed by the Conservatives. The nowadays little-known Campbell-Bannerman, whose portrait adorned Smuts's study ever after, *to all appearances an ordinary man, almost commonplace,*[58] became for Smuts the personification of a philosophy that irradiated his thinking on international affairs, the symbol of what was best and noblest in British statesmanship, the supreme example of what he called the *contagion of magnanimity.*[59] *They gave us back our country,* he marvelled, *in everything but name.*[60] Britain's magnanimity wiped out the *century of wrong.* Twelve years later, in November 1918, at the end of the First World War, Smuts recalled that *the greatest experience of my life* had been to see how, in South Africa, *a policy of reconciliation and trust recreated a land broken by war, and healed wounds and wrongs.*[61]

> They [the British] gave us back our country in everything but name. After four years. Has such a miracle of trust and magnanimity ever happened before?
>
> J C SMUTS

With the grant of self-government to the Transvaal, Het Volk won the ensuing election there in 1907. Botha and Smuts took office, Botha as Prime Minister and Smuts as Colonial Secretary and Minister of Education, in reality Botha's right-hand man. It was Smuts who laboured incessantly behind the scenes and it was his ability to execute government policy that made things happen. Smuts was immensely hardworking, a man of rapid decision-making and instant action. The longueurs of committees and parliamentary debate were a trial to him. He would listen impassively, only the drumming of his fingers betraying his impatience. He did not suffer fools gladly: *The dogs bark, but the caravan moves on,* he used to say.

Many thought him an unsocial figure, unapproachable and austere; but the frowning mien which he often assumed may have been intended to ward off unwelcome calls on his time. Serious-minded he was, but rarely sombre or gloomy. 'Vitality lifted the air as soon as he approached,'[62] writes his friend and biographer Sarah Millin, and he had a persuasive natural charm when it came to winning over an opponent or waiverer with an eager smile and a cheerful remark. *A smile is a healing process*,[63] he observed. With his buoyant self-confidence, boundless energy and constant zeal for work, Smuts was known to be the driving-force in Botha's government. A cartoon of a cabinet meeting shows six ministers, all with the face of Smuts. *All great men*, he once said, *are committees of one*.[64]

In contrast to Botha, benign and conciliatory, always ready for a game of bridge or a long chat over a pipe, Smuts never smoked, disdained cards, was impatient of small-talk and seldom sat still for long. Reluctant to delegate and with a certain dictatorial peremptoriness, he alienated his political adversaries and even his own colleagues. 'Slim Jannie' they called him – clever or crafty Jan – and the name stuck. *I am one of those shady politicians you hear about*,[65] he said, for he had an ironic sense of humour, often concealed by a poker-face, which non-plussed those who did not know him and convinced them that he was indeed 'slim'. Even when he went out of his way to be friendly, he did not always remove the suspicion that charm was part of his *slimness*.[66]

Smuts's most inveterate critic was Hertzog, who habitually accused him of selling out to the British. Two of six ministerial posts went to the English-speaking National Party and it was held against Smuts that he accepted the primacy of English in the Transvaal schools, Dutch being optional. His enemies also instanced his gift in 1907 to King Edward VII of the recently discovered Cullinan Diamond, the largest in the world, followed by his promotion the same year to King's Counsel. Smuts assured the Transvaal Parliament, to much laughter, that there was *no slimness*[67] about the gift!

The Union of South Africa

Smuts never lost sight of the wider vision with which first Rhodes and then Botha had inspired him: a united South Africa, *a union, not of top-dog and under-dog, but of brothers*,[68] in which the English-speaking states of Cape Colony and Natal and the Afrikaans-speaking Transvaal and Orange Free State should combine to form a Dominion of South Africa, which might itself eventually aspire to freedom from imperial tutelage. In 1908 Smuts took the first steps towards realising this ambition. He called a National Convention of all four colonies to discuss a constitution. His legal expertise and political skills now came fully into their own, for Smuts himself made the most active contribution to union, producing a variety of draft proposals for consideration by the 33 delegates to the Convention, sworn enemies only a few years before, whom he chivvied and cajoled into agreement on a final compromise. After a referendum in Natal, this was ratified by the Parliament of each colony. It was then approved by the Westminster Parliament and on 31 May 1910, eight years after Vereeniging and a week after Smuts's 40th birthday, the Union of South Africa was born.

South Africa was a unitary state created from the two English-speaking and the two Dutch-speaking colonies, each of which retained limited local powers of taxation and education. A bicameral Parliament (Assembly and Senate) sat at Cape Town, Pretoria became the seat of government, and ministers travelled the 1,000 miles from Pretoria to Cape Town and back again at the beginning and end of each parliamentary session. The Supreme Court sat at Bloemfontein. The first general election in the new Dominion took place in September 1910. Botha became Prime Minister as head of the South African National Party (later the South African Party), which he and Smuts formed out of Het Volk and other like-minded Boer and English-speaking parties. Hertzog joined the Government but resigned in 1912 to lead the Afrikaner National Party in opposition.

Smuts never claimed the full state allowances to which he was entitled, believing that public men should not touch public funds. Never affluent except in his early years at the Pretoria Bar, he was not interested in money as such. He lent freely and was seldom repaid. He bought a succession of farms, a dozen in all, three of which he worked and lived on. His favourite was Doornkloof (Thorn Valley), which he bought in 1908. Doornkloof was situated on the high veld near the village of Irene, 10 miles from Pretoria. The house, formerly a temporary British officers' mess, was a prefabricated structure of wood and corrugated iron which Smuts transported and erected at Doornkloof. Stifling in summer, cold and drafty in winter, Doornkloof, wrote Smuts's son, was 'an ideal refuge for stoics'.[69] Smuts's main luxury was his well-stocked library, the sanctuary where he immersed himself in his scholarly interests. *This*, he said, *is a place for enquiry.*[70] Only the babble of the children at play disturbed his concentration, yet he would complain both when they broke the silence and when they did not.

He borrowed on the security of his farms and lived off overdrafts for his outgoings and book purchases. Isie, who kept the accounts which he could not be bothered to attend to, warned him that the farms were unprofitable; but Smuts took little notice. He relished the old patriarchal life of the Boer farmer, or at least the illusion of that life: for he hired managers to run the farms whether the farms paid their way or not, and his prize herd of pedigree Friesians, which he delighted in showing to visitors at Doornkloof, was as much a luxury as his library. Both to his black farm workers and his family he was known by an endearing and respectful Afrikaans form of address as the *Oubaas*, the Old Boss or Master, and to his friends as *Oom Jannie* – Uncle Jannie. This self-styled farmer disliked dogs and was no handyman: he was never seen about the house with hammer or screwdriver, and his slender hands and long tapering fingers suggested the artist rather than a man of the soil. His motoring, which he much enjoyed, was hair-raising. He would race along at break-neck speed, indifferent to road signs or other drivers, turning around to address his passengers in the back and taking his hands off the wheel to emphasize some point with a danger-ously expansive gesture. 'O.J.'s driving always put the wind up me,'[71] a typical passenger recalled.

Doornkloof was Smuts's retreat for 40 years. *Isn't this wonderful!*[72] he exclaimed whenever he returned home. There he was at his happiest, among his family and his books. He resumed poetry reading and *Lieder*-singing with Isie. He delighted in boisterous games with the children (and later the grandchildren), in studying the local birdlife, and the plants and grasses, which he collected assiduously and on which he became an expert. He found paleo-botany *one of the most enthralling things in the world.*[73] A visiting lady botanist from America, astonished at his encyclopaedic knowledge, asked how the General found time for it. *Madam*, replied Smuts, *I am a General only in my spare time.*[74] He was never idle, always ready for long excursions on horseback or on foot, when his juniors had difficulty in keeping up with his rapid stride. He would take a dip in a mountain pool or, at Cape Town, he would swim out to sea, careless of treacherous cur-rents. But his favourite and habitual relaxation there was to climb Table Mountain. High above the city and the ocean, he attained a sense of renewal and exhilaration, of serene detachment and oneness with nature and *that silent sympathy and communion which she alone can give.*[75] He spoke later of *the religion of the mountain.*[76]

As before, Smuts, now Minister of the Interior, of Defence and of Mines, was Botha's ubiquitous assistant, and he was personally responsible for devising and setting up much of South Africa's legal and administrative system. During Botha's absence in London at the Imperial Defence Conference of 1911, he was acting Prime Minister. As Minister of Defence, he drafted the 1912 Defence Act, which established the South African army, or Union Defence Force – the 'Springboks'. As Minister of Mines, he introduced safety regulations and also entrenched the colour bar in the mining industry.

The franchise was the most sensitive domestic political issue in South Africa. From the first, the Union was avowedly based on white supremacy. Smuts accepted as a fact of life the Boer refusal to recognise the black man as an equal. Neither in the Transvaal nor in the Orange Free State were blacks enfranchised. In the Cape Province, the Prime Minister, John Merriman, favoured a continuation of the limited franchise that prevailed there, based on property and education, for black and white alike. The British government had intended to extend this franchise throughout the Union. Smuts was willing for the arrangement in the Cape to remain as it was; but he knew his Afrikaners, and in his overriding preoccupation to unite Briton and Boer, he was clear that *public opinion in the majority of the South African states is against a native franchise in any shape or form*[77] and that a broader solution must be put off to the remote future. *We are a small white colony in a Dark Continent,*[78] he reminded Parliament in

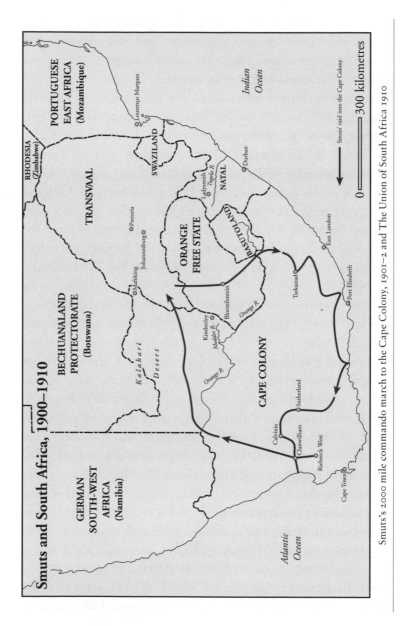

Smuts's 2000 mile commando march to the Cape Colony, 1901–2 and The Union of South Africa 1910

1914. The Natives Land Act 1913 restricted land ownership by blacks to 7 per cent of the country.

The same Boer attitude went for other races. Milner's introduction of Chinese labour in the mines had provoked strong indignation. Smuts was determined that the Chinese should leave, and leave they did. There was also a 150,000-strong Indian minority in South Africa, and it was there that their spokesman, Mohandas Gandhi, waged his first campaign of passive resistance. Smuts, who had introduced legislation to limit Indian immigration in the Transvaal, applied the same policy throughout the Union. On a personal level, Smuts had a high regard for Gandhi, whose spirituality appealed to his own. But engrossed in *the task of welding the old Colonies into a unified State*, he found Gandhi's activities *very trying*, not least since *Gandhi raised a most troublesome issue*, the issue of race. *We had*, he admitted, *a skeleton in our cupboard.*[79]

Syndicalism, a form of militant class-warfare, was rife among South Africa's white labour force. A miners' strike erupted on the Rand in 1913. Rioting and arson broke out and spread to Johannesburg. Smuts and Botha agreed to negotiate with the (mainly English) strike-leaders but were forced to capitulate to their threats. Smuts bided his time and prepared for a showdown. When the miners stepped up their demands and attempted to repeat their success in January 1914 by calling a general strike, Smuts hit back hard. *The country*, he said, *was face to face with a revolution.*[80] He declared martial law, called in the Union Defence Force and shipped the strike leaders back to England before a writ of *habeas corpus* could be served. His action, sharp, decisive and admittedly unlawful – Parliament passed an act of indemnity to protect him – showed a side of Smuts that gave grounds for the view of him, if not as 'slim', then certainly as fearless and resolute.

2

War and Peace: 1914–18

Britain's declaration of war on Germany in August 1914 automatically brought the Empire, including the new South Africa, into the struggle. *What times we live in and what fate is in store for our day and generation,*[1] Smuts wrote prophetically to Wolstenholme, his old Cambridge tutor. To Arthur Gillett he wrote of his attitude to Germany: *I love German thought and culture and hope it will yet do much for mankind. But a stern limit must be set to her political system, which is a menace to the world even worse than Bonapartism was.*[2] But the War proved highly divisive in South Africa. It reopened scars barely a dozen years old. Hertzog and the Afrikaner National Party advocated neutrality. 'We are not pro-German but anti-British,'[3] said Hertzog, but a German victory would offer the prospect of shaking off the British yoke and reversing the outcome of the Boer War.

Smuts, however, declared unequivocally: *Botha and I are not the men to desert England in this dark hour,*[4] and Parliament supported them. With Turkey an ally of Germany, the route to India and Australia via the Suez Canal was at risk and the route around the Cape of Good Hope resumed its former importance. Botha was asked to eliminate the threat to communications from the naval bases and wireless stations in German South-West Africa (now Namibia).

Even as Botha and Smuts drew up invasion plans, however, 12,000 Boer War veterans in the Union Defence Force, including its own commanders General Christian Beyers in the Transvaal and General de Wet in the Orange Free State, resigned their commissions, crossed into South-West Africa and raised the standard of rebellion against the Union. Some defected to the Germans, for Kaiser Wilhelm II promised support. Smuts took over personal command of the Union Defence Force and declared martial law, while Botha moved successfully against the rebels. Beyers fled and was drowned while attempting to cross the Vaal. Another defector, Smuts's former Boer War comrade and political colleague, General Koos de la Rey – *we were almost brothers*,[5] wrote Smuts – was accidently shot dead. Most of the captured rebels were let off lightly but a Major Jopie Fourie, who joined the rebels without resigning his commission and in full South African uniform, was captured after an engagement in which a dozen soldiers were treacherously killed when he opened fire under a flag of truce. Fourie was brought before a court martial. One of its members asked to be excused because he was a friend of Fourie. *I replied that that was an additional reason why he should serve*, said Smuts. The court was unanimous and Fourie was sentenced to death. Smuts refused a reprieve and let the sentence stand: *I would have shirked my duty if I had not*,[6] he maintained; but Fourie, who faced the firing-squad with great courage, became a Boer folk-hero and martyr while Smuts, labelled 'murderer of Fourie' by his Afrikaner foes, became *the best-hated man in South Africa*.[7]

German Africa

The mutiny over, in March 1915 Botha invaded German South-West Africa from the north, Smuts from the south. Disregarding textbook tactics and with the same flair he had once shown against the British, Smuts outmanoeuvred the Germans in a lightning advance on horseback across 700 miles of the Kalahari Desert. The thinly-held territory was rapidly overcome, the Germans surrendered, and Botha and Smuts were back in the Union by July. In the rowdy general election of October, violently contested by Hertzog's Nationalists, shots were fired. Smuts narrowly escaped being hit and the South Africa Party lost its overall majority.

Smuts waged war but he was no warmonger. Rather he saw himself as a man *who in these times is forced to do soldiering against his will.*[8] He was profoundly aware of the disaster that had befallen civilization with the advent of total, industrialised warfare. At Christmas 1915, he wrote to Arthur Gillett: *It is terrible and depressing to see all the great discoveries and scientific achievements of our race turned like so many daggers against the heart of the race.*[9] To Wolstenholme, he wrote: *Will mankind, sick of all this horror, turn inward and purify its spirit, or will it become debased and demoralized and brutalized by its horrible experience?*[10]

In February 1916, at Britain's request, Smuts took command of the 45,000 Imperial troops bogged down in a costly and failing campaign in German East Africa (Tanganyika, now Tanzania), *the jewel of the German colonial empire.*[11] With the rank of Lieutenant-General, the second youngest general in the British army, he led a polyglot force including 20,000 South Africans. German East Africa was vast, inhospitable and disease-ridden. For every one of his men injured in battle, 30 fell sick from disease. Smuts himself came down with malaria, from which he never wholly recovered. Dosing himself with quinine, he forced himself to carry on. The campaign was plagued by torrential rain: *I have never in all my life dreamt that rain could fall as it does here,* he wrote. *The country is one vast swamp.*[12]

In this tropical hell-hole Smuts contended with the resourceful German General, Paul Emil von Lettow-Vorbeck, whose orders were to resist at all costs. Lettow-Vorbeck evaded outright defeat; but in a 10-month campaign marked by a characteristic combination of speed and surprise, Smuts edged him into an ever-contracting hinterland, while he himself gained control of a huge territory extending from the foothills of Mount Kilimanjaro in the north to the River Rufiji in the south, and west to east from the Great Lakes to the Indian Ocean. By January 1917 Smuts had fulfilled his instructions to the letter, though Lettow-Vorbeck held out until after the Armistice.

As in the Boer War and in South-West Africa, Smuts showed himself a shrewd and far-sighted strategist, a bold and imaginative tactician and an inspiring leader who drove himself as hard as any of his men, painstaking in reconnaissance, always visibly active and in the thick of things. South African casualties – 2,100 dead – were relatively low, but Smuts was accused by his own chief of intelligence of recklessness and poor generalship, a charge which he rejected. *I could have played for safety,* he said, *but at what cost would I have done so! A timid Fabian strategy would, of all, have been the most fatal in this country and against this enemy. ... The commander who shrinks from such efforts should stay at home.*[13] With his record and with such an attitude, Smuts inspired his men with faith in his lucky star. 'In this war and with this General,' wrote one of them, 'nothing was impossible.'[14] As in the Boer War, Smuts also displayed a fine sense of chivalry. When the Kaiser awarded Lettow-Vorbeck the Iron Cross, it fell into Smuts's hands. Smuts forwarded it to Lettow-Vorbeck with his congratulations.

Smuts in Britain

After the campaign, Smuts was recalled to South Africa. His spectacular success, uniquely welcome in a War marked in the European theatre so far by almost unrelieved failure for the Allies, had not escaped the notice of Lloyd George. Newly come to power as a Prime Minister pledged to decisive victory, Lloyd George invited the Dominion leaders, whose contribution to the War was proving all-important, to attend a conference in London. Two kinds of conference were in fact under way simultaneously. One was an Imperial War Conference which, following the pattern of similar pre-war gatherings, discussed relations between Britain and the Dominions and constitutional matters. The other was the newly created Imperial War Cabinet, chaired by the Prime Minister and attended by the Dominion heads, which co-ordinated war policy. Botha, who felt he could not leave South Africa and whose English did not compare with that of Smuts, sent Smuts to England in his stead.

Kitchener, Minister of War until his death the year before, had sourly predicted that 'My generals,' who had fought Smuts in the Boer War, 'will not accept Mr Smuts.'[15] He could not have been further from the truth. From the moment of his arrival in England in March 1917 Smuts received a hero's welcome across the country. There was talk of re-naming German East Africa 'Smutsland'. Military men, politicians, society and the public lionized him, for, as Winston Churchill said, Smuts was 'the only one who is fresh and

'One knew of the General's daring and brilliant strategy, of his amazing feats of warfare, of his hairbreadth escapes. One knew of him as a profound and learned lawyer of varied experience. One recognised in him a statesman of marvellous insight and resources. Yet he stood there, an active soldier, without any sign of care or anxiety or endurance with a dancing light of gaiety and interest in his eyes, his small mobile lips uttering those simple and graceful sentences, but without preoccupation or nervousness, or anxiety as to how his words would be received ... He seemed to me the embodiment of grace and sympathy and freedom. He had no touch of resentment or suspicion about him. He was not there to conciliate or to ingratiate himself or to persuade. He was just a friend among friends, entirely trustful and kindly and grateful ... and with all misunderstanding and hostility and passion swept away.'

A C BENSON, MASTER OF MAGDALENE COLLEGE, CAMBRIDGE, ON J C SMUTS'S VISIT TO HIS OLD COLLEGE, CHRIST'S COLLEGE, MAY 1917[16]

bright, unwounded mentally and physically'.[17] He met his old adversary, Milner, at a dinner. An onlooker recalled 'Smuts, slipping his arm into Milner's as they walked out of the dining-room'.[18] Smuts quickly established his pre-eminence among his fellow colonials. Ex-Prime Minister Asquith saw in him 'a man of first-rate ability, head and shoulders above the rest of the Dominions representatives'.[19] At a dinner in the Middle Temple, his host, Lord Shaw, raised with Smuts a case of the highest constitutional importance on which he was then engaged affecting the liberty of the subject. Smuts 'saw the crux of the case in a moment' and referred Shaw to a key precedent which determined Shaw's decision in the case. 'I turned up the Reports,' Shaw noted, 'and found that he was right in every particular.' 'As our guest,' added Shaw, 'he won all hearts.'[20]

Moved as he was by his reception, Smuts also had his own agenda. His enemies at home had jeered that he considered South Africa too small for him. This he denied. *Every drop of blood and every bit of courage and determination I have in me*, he declared, *will go to the service of my country.*[21] He soon showed that this was not empty heroics. To Isie he wrote of his determination *to see that in future our position in the Dominions is improved. I cannot and never shall forget that we were free republics.*[22] Ideas were afoot of imperial federation, the object of Milner and his 'kindergarten'; but Smuts saw such tightening of links as a threat to South Africa's freedom of action, and he argued skilfully and successfully for a far looser relationship between Britain and *the Dominions as autonomous nations of an Imperial Commonwealth.*[23] The concept, and the very name 'the British Commonwealth of Nations', was launched by Smuts in a speech to members of both Houses of Parliament in May 1917 which completely routed the federalists. His scheme became the forerunner of the Statute of Westminster (1931) and a milestone in the political emancipation of the Dominions.

Lloyd George was quick to perceive Smuts's remarkable qualities: vision and imagination, practicality, boundless energy and zeal. When the Imperial War Cabinet was dissolved in June, Lloyd George prevailed on him to remain in England and to join the War Cabinet proper, the Prime Minister's inner Cabinet and supreme executive body in the waging of the War. Here, as a Minister without Portfolio, Smuts sat with Lloyd George, Lord Curzon (Lord President of the

Council), Andrew Bonar Law (Chancellor of the Exchequer), Lord Milner (Minister without Portfolio), Austen Chamberlain (Secretary of State for India) and George Barnes (Labour Party representative and Minister without Portfolio). Such an appointment was unprecedented for someone not a member of either House of Parliament, for Smuts turned down Lloyd George's suggestion that he stand for Parliament. As South Africa's Minister of Defence, he scrupulously refused an additional salary.

Smuts was housed at the Savoy Hotel, but lived with his customary frugality. He preferred to chew a strip of 'biltong', dried meat which Isie sent out from South Africa, to the sumptuous fare provided; and while Lloyd George repaired to an underground shelter during German air-raids on London, Smuts would go up to the roof of the Savoy to watch the bombers overhead and brave their lethal payload. C P Scott, editor of the *Manchester Guardian*, found him 'a very charming person, perfectly simple, sincere and modest'. He was, Scott noted, 'in ordinary officer's khaki, without a scrap of decoration – gold or red tab – he might have passed for the least distinguished of the soldiers present. ... Obviously a very big man.' [24] A year later, when King George V made him a Privy Councillor and first of the newly created Companions of Honour, Smuts was embarrassed. *These things do go against my Boer grain*,[25] he wrote, though he would receive many honours in his time. Chaim Weizmann, a leading British Zionist, broaching with him the cause of a Jewish homeland in Palestine to which Smuts became a ready convert, noted that 'a sort of warmth of understanding radiated from him'.[26] Smuts had a natural dignity and an unaffected cordiality, which, however suspiciously viewed by his Boer adversaries at home, served him well in Britain. 'He has that wonderful trick of never forgetting faces or names',[27] an observer noted. C P Scott told Lloyd George in September 1917 that 'Smuts was perhaps the most popular man in the country'.[28]

At the same time Smuts also made contact with his old friends, Alice Clark, and the Gilletts at Oxford. Forsaking the company of the statesmen, civil servants, politicians and magnates with whom he engaged during the week, he regularly sought the hospitality of these friends at weekends, finding among them rest, recreation and solace. 102 Banbury Road, he wrote later, *has done more for me than the War Cabinet or any other of the great institutions of England.*[29] He loved the simplicity of their life and faith, he felt relaxed and at ease with them, and while they radically disagreed about the War, he was ethically and spiritually attuned to their values. His 'holistic' leanings impelled him to try and reconcile the War in which he was doing his utmost for the British cause with their unshakeable Quaker pacifism. Despite the terrible ordeal which the world was undergoing, he felt that this was a just war. He saw himself as being *on active service for humanity,*[30] and as he wrote to Wolstenholme, *I have faith in the ultimate Good of the Universe.*[31] The Clarks believed that no war was just; their menfolk were conscientious objectors and three Clark cousins were in gaol for their convictions. Smuts had been a soldier, as he said, for one-sixth of his life, but his friends' pacifism gave sustenance to his own ultimate vision, which was against war. He became a prominent advocate of the idea of a League of Nations as an institution that should outlaw resort to war. A resolution drafted by him and approved by the Imperial War Cabinet in April 1917 affirmed that some scheme for the resolution of *international disputes not susceptible to arbitration or judicial procedure ...*

should be discussed with our allies and especially the USA and embodied in the peace treaty itself.[32]

His abhorrence of war, of the slaughter of *the best – the very best*[33] by the *horrible engine of destruction*, was manifest from his public speeches. *After all the fair promises, all the fair hopes, all the fine enthusiasm of the nineteenth century, this is what we have come to*, he lamented in a speech in May 1917 to launch a League of Nations Society. He feared that the end of the War would see *an atmosphere of hatred and ill-will and of international estrangement;*[34] yet he insisted that Britain was *not inspired by any vengeful feelings, by a desire to destroy the German nation,*[35] and would in the end *make a wise settlement, not only in its own interests but in the interests of the whole of Europe.*[36] In the same speech he welcomed President Wilson's support for the idea of a League as *a union of free peoples for the preservation of permanent peace.*[37]

One observer thought Smuts superior to any member of the War Cabinet for 'pure intellect', the ability to penetrate to the heart of a subject, coupled with the 'still rarer quality' of 'being able to state clearly what he has seen'.[38] Smuts argued that while Germany was so far undeniably victorious on the Continent, the winner over the rest of the globe was Britain, whose overseas gains were unassailable: thanks to the Royal Navy, they could not be wrested from her. From the first he was adamant that the conquered German colonies should be retained. Their possession was *an achievement of enormous value which ought not to be endangered at the peace negotiations.*[39] Any notion of restoring South-West Africa to Germany was *absolutely impossible.*[40] It would weaken the South African Party, strengthen the Afrikaner opposition and *jeopardise the whole position in South Africa* so recently settled. A resurgent Germany would turn the colony into a launch-pad for land, sea and air attacks on South Africa. German East Africa should likewise be retained for *the safety of the British Empire as a whole*[41] and as the main link in Rhodes's old vision of a continuous chain of British territory from the Cape to Cairo.

As the only member of the War Cabinet to have commanded in the field, Smuts was consulted on the strategy of the War. In April 1917 he was sent by Lloyd George to sound out feeling among the Allied commanders in France and Belgium. In June, he was appointed to the newly established Cabinet War Committee, whose members included the British Commander-in-Chief, Sir Douglas Haig. Smuts, like Lloyd George, voiced his mistrust of Haig's insistence on a preponderant Allied commitment to the Western Front. *I have no confidence that we can break through the enemy line on any large scale,* he declared, *in a theatre mainly of the enemy's choosing,* where the British and French armies were *locked up in front of almost impregnable positions.*[42]

Smuts nonetheless persuaded a sceptical War Cabinet to approve Haig's proposed campaign in Flanders, aimed at driving the Germans from their submarine bases at Zeebrugge and Ostend. He bitterly regretted his decision when the campaign degenerated into the prolonged bloodbath of Passchendaele, for he had given his sanction on the understanding that Haig would call off the offensive unless it achieved immediate success; yet he later reflected that despite its terrible cost, it had prevented a French collapse and the loss of the War. Lloyd George later sent Smuts on a fruitless mission to British headquarters in France to ascertain whether there was anyone capable of replacing Haig, that *unimaginative man,*[43] as Smuts called him. In November 1917 after the disastrous rout of the Italian army at Caporetto, Smuts accompanied Lloyd George to a conference at Rapallo, where he supported the Prime Minister's plan to rush British troops to Italy's assistance lest she pull out of the War as Russia had done.

In December 1917, travelling incognito as 'Mr Smith', Smuts was sent on a secret mission to Switzerland to explore the possibility of a separate peace with Austria-Hungary. His talks at Geneva with Count Albert von Mensdorff, formerly Austrian Ambassador to London, and three months later with a second Austrian emissary, showed such hopes to be vain: Austria was tied helplessly to Germany; but the talks did suggest to Smuts the desirability of clarifying Britain's War aims and of making it plain that these did not include the break-up of Germany. Smuts's draft was among those on which Lloyd George based his important War-aims speech of 5 January 1918, a few days before the still more momentous Fourteen Points speech of President Wilson. So highly did Lloyd George rate Smuts's abilities that he considered making him Foreign Secretary. Smuts, he said, would be the 'ideal man'.[44]

Lloyd George had offered Smuts command of the campaign against the Turks in Palestine, *the last and greatest Crusade*,[45] which on his reluctant refusal (he felt that lacking the support of the War Office, it would turn into a secondary side-show) went to General Edmund Allenby; but in February 1918 he was sent to Egypt and Palestine, where he took part in planning Allenby's successful advance on Damascus. Smuts favoured the Zionist cause in Palestine. A friend of Weizmann, he was a signatory and lifelong partisan of the Balfour Declaration, which designated Palestine as 'a national home for the Jewish people'. He saw for himself the barren hills of Judaea and he looked forward to a day when the vine and the olive would cover them as in biblical times.

Smuts had enormous admiration for Lloyd George as a war leader, describing him (in words that apply equally to Smuts himself) as *brilliant, energetic, resourceful and courageous without limit*.[46] In April 1918 the British Army was reeling under the Ludendorff offensive. It was the gravest crisis of the War. Smuts, who had foreseen the offensive and the points on the British line where it would fall, wrote to Lloyd George to express his confidence in victory notwithstanding *these days of supreme peril*.[47]

In June 1918 Smuts made the unlikely suggestion to Lloyd George that he be put in overall command of the American Army in France, disappointingly inactive under General John Joseph Pershing, whom he described as *very commonplace*.[48] Smuts yearned to lead the Americans in an offensive capacity to help the hard-pressed Allies. He opposed Allied intervention in Russia where the despatch of Allied forces, originally intended to prevent war-supplies there from falling into German hands, was taking on the appearance of an anti-Bolshevik crusade. Smuts feared that *the consequences were incalculable*, perhaps *the beginning of a new war ... The time must come when Russia would recover. What would be her feeling towards us if in her day of weakness we had assisted in her dismemberment?*[49]

Lloyd George also entrusted Smuts with a variety of assignments on the home front. He was a versatile trouble-shooter, who, as the Prime Minister commented, 'could be safely entrusted to examine into the intricacies of any of the multifarious war problems, and unravel and smooth them out'.[50] However, Smuts turned down the chairmanship of the Irish Convention, set up by Lloyd George at Smuts's suggestion in the aftermath of the 1916 Easter Rebellion. The Convention was intended to induce the Irish to settle their political differences as the South Africans had done at their Convention in 1908. Smuts certainly agreed on the urgent need for a solution. 'As to Ireland', noted C P Scott, 'he regarded it as essential to settle before the Peace Conference. How could we go into the Peace Conference with "*this skeleton in the cupboard*" still on our hands? "*We ... had settled South Africa and we must settle Ireland*".'[51] Smuts urged Lloyd George to abandon any solution based on Home Rule, a lost cause since the Rebellion. Nor, despite the dire pressure of the Ludendorff offensive, should he think of introducing Irish conscription: mere *tomfoolery*, he said, *in the present temper of Ireland*, likely to provoke civil war at the most desperate moment of the War, when the Allies were struggling to hold back the German advance and *fighting for our life*.[52]

In September 1917 Smuts became chairman of the important War Priorities Committee of the War Cabinet, set up at his suggestion to deal with the allocation of resources between competing departments. 'He was the most efficient hustler when he liked',[53] a colleague noted, but the work was daunting. *I have never worked so hard in my life*, he said later. *My hair became white*.[54] Not the least of his services was as a regular public speaker, a champion of the Allied cause, confident throughout the darkest days of the War in ultimate victory. In October 1917 Lloyd George sent him to quell a miners' strike in South Wales. Acting on a tip from Lloyd George as he faced the massed ranks of sullen workers, he first invited them to sing. This was a call which no Welshmen could resist, and after an emotional rendering of 'Land of My Fathers' and a few words from Smuts, the strike was over.

Of great long-term significance was Smuts's response, at Lloyd George's request, to London's vulnerability to German air raids. Smuts recommended not only a variety of measures to protect the capital but also the establishment of the Royal Air Force as an independent branch of the armed services. He saw air power as a formidable offensive arm that could carry the fight into the German heartland at a time when the Allied Armies were only just beginning to stem, with painful slowness and high casualties, the German advance. Thousands of aircraft rolled off the stocks for deployment in the mass bombing of Germany planned for 1919. Smuts's doctrine of the superior destructive capacity of air power would be followed for good or ill in the Second World War.

Smuts never shared Lloyd George's belief in the 'knockout blow', however. In a speech in May 1918 he doubted that out-and-out victory over the Central Powers was possible or even desirable. To *smash Germany* and dictate terms at Berlin would require *an interminable campaign*[55] of many years, would weaken Britain and destroy what was left of European civilisation. Across the continent, he warned, *the grim spectre of Bolshevist anarchy is stalking.*[56] Smuts had no sympathy for Bolshevism, though he understood its causes: it was *a disease of socialism arising from the horrors and sufferings of this war, but still a disease.*[57] He also feared the fragmentation of Central and Eastern Europe: that *the more or less orderly* state system of 1914 would give way to *a wild disorder of jarring and warring state fragments*[58] as nation-states splintered off from the Russian and Austro-Hungarian Empires right across Europe. What was to *prevent a wild war-dance of these so-called free nations?*[59] As late as October 1918, Smuts believed the War might go on until 1920. *Was that worth while?*[60] he asked the War Cabinet. When it became clear that Germany was in fact close to collapse, Smuts argued strongly for a ceasefire while Britain was still in a position to influence the peace terms. *If peace comes now, it will be a British peace,*[61] he said, but the longer the war continued, the more the balance of power would favour America. Eventually America *would dictate to the world.*[62]

Dining at 10 Downing Street with Lloyd George, Churchill and the Attorney-General Sir Frederick Smith (later Lord Chancellor Birkenhead) on the eve of the Armistice, he urged the Prime Minister *to be large and generous and to send food at once to the famished millions on the Continent.*[63] The four men discussed sending food ships to Hamburg. Such an act, said Smuts, an impulse of *simple human feelings*, would *help to purify and sweeten* an atmosphere *cursed with war, hate and untruth.*[64] That night he wrote with fervour: *May God in this great hour remove from us all smallness of heart and vitalize our souls with sympathy and fellow-feeling for those in affliction – the beaten, the weak and the little ones who have no food.*[65] But the blockade would not be fully lifted for over half a year.

Louis Botha by Sir William Orpen (1919). Botha felt almost as strongly as Smuts about the Treaty of Versailles, but felt he must sign 'because', as he cabled the Governor-General of South Africa on 23 June 1919, 'my position as Prime Minister is different from his, and my signature is necessary to make [the] Union a member of the League of Nations and secure for her a new status in the world'.

II
The Paris Peace Conference

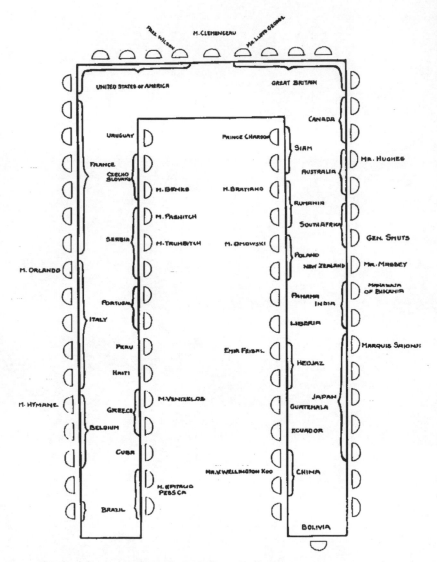

Sketch of the seating plan at the Paris Peace Conference.

3
Peacemaking: November 1918– February 1919

The Armistice brought no respite for Smuts. Lloyd George had entrusted him with the task of drafting the outlines of British policy at the Peace Conference. He was also working on an important memorandum on the League of Nations, as well as making a case for Dominion representation at the Conference and setting out South Africa's territorial claims. He still sat as a member of the War Cabinet and he chaired its Demobilisation Committee. 'He never did anything,' wrote a colleague, 'comparable to his work during November 1918.'[1]

'Our Policy at the Peace Conference' was a concise summary of Britain's post-war priorities. Smuts urged alignment with America rather than with France, *a bad neighbour to us in the past*, who would *do her best to remain mistress of the Continent*.[2] This was a somewhat cynical view of Britain's closest ally, but it also reflected Lloyd George's attitude once the War was over. As he had advocated during the War, Smuts placed the establishment of a League of Nations at the heart of the Conference agenda. Here his thinking was closer to that of Woodrow Wilson. Like Wilson, Smuts saw the League as *not merely a formula, but a real substantive part of our future international system* and *the key to most of the new troubles.*[3]

Smuts's mood at the Armistice was one of pride and optimism. He admired British sobriety in the hour of victory: *no hymns of hate, no trampling on a prostrate foe.*[4] Three days after the Armistice he made an important speech to a gathering of American newspaper editors, in which he appealed for Anglo-American cooperation in *the great creative tasks ahead of us.* He urged that peacemaking be conducted in the spirit of *this moral idealism and this vision of a better world* that had sustained Britain during the War. *The downfall of Prussian militarism* should be followed by the creation of a League of Nations *which will secure us against a recurrence of such disasters in future.*[5]

He saw the immediate problems facing the Allies as practical and humanitarian: the restoration of *Europe, of broken and bleeding Europe, the mother of our common civilisation.*[6] Disorder was rife and revolution threatened to engulf the continent. Bolshevism was no answer to Europe's ills. *You cannot save mankind by barring the élite and letting the proletariat run riot,*[7] he wrote to Alice Clark; and by the provision of aid to Central and Eastern Europe he sought to remedy the destruction, starvation and despair on which Bolshevism fed.

Smuts emphasised in his speech the realities of Europe that would preoccupy him throughout the Conference. The Europe of 1914 was in dissolution – *a whole world order is visibly passing away before our eyes*[8] – as former subject peoples asserted their right to self-determination as independent states. The western fringes of the Russian Empire had already broken away. The Ottoman (Turkish) Empire had fallen apart. The Austro-Hungarian Empire was in the throes of disintegration.

Amid this fluid and turbulent chaos, Smuts identified three cardinal facts. First, the collapse of the old balance of power, the system of mutual deterrence through rival power-blocs by which the Great Powers had traditionally kept the peace in Europe. The Entente (Britain, France and Russia) had, albeit precariously, counterbalanced the Central Powers (Germany and Austria-Hungary) from around the turn of the century until 1914, when the deterrent failed; and then the War destroyed the old Russia and Austria-Hungary. Coupled with the ensuing power-vacuum on the continent was the second problem highlighted by Smuts: the threat of chronic instability posed by the fragmentation (or 'Balkanisation') of Eastern and Central Europe. Lastly there was the survival, amid the disintegration and disorder surrounding her, of a united Germany. The fate of the continent would depend on the interaction of all three of these factors; and the overriding challenge awaiting the Peace Conference was to recognise and to act on the need to reconcile Germany and *the new Europe*[9] for their mutual and common salvation.

Smuts spelled out the prospect of Europe's fragmentation. *From Finland in the north to Constantinople in the south*, he said, *the map of Europe will be covered with small nations*. Their problems were many and daunting. All were *in a state of destitution*. Most were *untrained in habits of self-government*. Most contained *a resolute minority of alien race making for internal weakness*. Nearly all were *divided from each other by profound national or racial prejudices and antipathies*,[10] with the danger of fresh quarrels and hostilities inherent at their very birth. Against this background of weakness, instability and mutual mistrust was the fact of a

German state in the heart of Europe, strengthened by *racial homogeneity* and by *education and political discipline*.[11]

Smuts thus recognised and articulated with great clarity the geopolitical facts that would underlie any settlement, whatever schemes the peacemakers might propose or devise. He put his finger on these realities and kept it there throughout the Conference. After the terrible ordeal of total war there was a natural feeling among the Allied peoples, once the immediate relief of the ceasefire had passed, that the hour of retribution had come, a common reaction that Germany should be cut down to size, made to pay for her misdeeds and incapacitated from repeating them. *It would all have been so much easier if Germany had put up a clean fight*, Smuts agreed. *But even so we have to be influenced by larger considerations*.[12]

Smuts recognised that to *hard-headed politicians and European diplomatists* the idea of a League of Nations appeared *utopian*,[13] but he argued that the establishment of such an organisation was indispensable: first and foremost to save Europe from immediate disaster, to coordinate measures for the relief of starvation, to recharge economies and get people back to work. Viewed in this light, *a League of Nations is no longer an ideal or an aspiration, but a sheer practical necessity*.[14] Above and beyond that, he portrayed a League of Nations as an instrument essential for the prevention of war in a Europe containing even more flashpoints than in 1914. The League must *take the place of the Great Powers which have disappeared and keep the peace among these smaller states.* He expressed confidence in its future: the League would *develop vitality, it will take root and grow.* He saw it as *the greatest creative effort of the human race in the sphere of political government*, which alone could justify *all the losses and sufferings of this, the greatest tragedy in history.*[15]

On 14 December 1918, when polling began in the British general election, Smuts scrupulously resigned from the War Cabinet. Two days later he completed his memorandum on the League, which was published in the new year as *The League of Nations: a Practical Suggestion*. Earlier ideas for a League had been drafted by Lord Robert Cecil and later by Lord Phillimore, a jurist. But Lloyd George had asked Smuts to look at the matter afresh and to produce the blueprint for a coherent and comprehensive scheme. The result, said Lloyd George, was 'one of the ablest state papers he had read'.[16]

Smuts's pamphlet fleshed out the ideas which he had outlined in his speech to the American newspapermen. As then, he presented the League as an instrument absolutely necessary to maintain peace in the new Europe: while *in the past the empires kept the peace among their rival nationalities, the League will have to keep the peace among the new states formed from these nationalities*; for without the League *the danger of future wars will be actually greater because of the multitudinous discordant states*, prone, as he said, *to fly at one another's throats. The new Europe* would present a huge challenge to the League in its task of *conciliating and composing differences between* them. The internecine history of the Balkan states before 1914 suggested the magnitude of that task and was a reminder of *the risk of a similar state of affairs arising on a much larger scale in the new Europe, covered as it will be with small independent states.*[17] This was to leave aside the still *more difficult question of the maintenance of future world peace* and how, in accordance with the 14th Point of President Wilson, *to guarantee the weak against the strong.*[18]

In words that thrilled and inspired Wilson himself, Smuts declared: *Europe is being liquidated, and the League of Nations must be the heir to this great estate.* By this he meant the management of territories and peoples liberated by the collapse of Russia, Austria-Hungary and Turkey. Fearing a *scramble among the victors for the loot*, Smuts argued that *reversion to the League of Nations should be substituted for any policy of national annexation*, or, as he put it, *a return of the old policy of grab and greed and partitions.* The League should take responsibility for the new states, which *are mostly destitute and will require much nursing towards economic and political independence.*[19]

While such new states as Finland, Poland, Czechoslovakia and Yugoslavia might look to the League for humanitarian and economic aid, their political independence should be recognised. Other states, on the margins of or outside Europe, should be assigned by the League to the tutelage of particular Powers, who would act as 'Mandatories' – agents or trustees of the League for the benefit of those states. Smuts had in mind such vulnerable regions as the former Russian dependencies of Georgia and Armenia and Middle East territories formerly under Turkish rule: Mesopotamia (Iraq), Syria, Lebanon and Palestine.

Smuts also drew up a constitution for the League. There should be a General Assembly, the forum for the discussion of international problems by member-states; but Smuts was determined that the League should be no mere *talking shop* or *futile debating society.*[20] At its core should be a standing Council of the Great Powers, where *the real work of the League*[21] would be done; a permanent Secretariat and permanent Courts of Arbitration and Conciliation. Smuts included provision for disarmament and mechanisms for the

'I have never read any State Paper ... with anything like the agreement I feel in regard to this of yours. I feel quite confident that President Wilson will agree with you. His language is wholly in that spirit. And I think you will find that you have expressed in definite proposals the hopes and aspirations prevalent in this country ... This war, terrible as it has been and irreparable as must be the mischief it has produced, will leave one compensation if your ideas are embodied in the results of the Peace Conference.'

EX-LORD CHANCELLOR LORD LOREBURN TO J C SMUTS, 22 DECEMBER 1918, ON THE LEAGUE OF NATIONS: A PRACTICAL SOLUTION[22]

prevention of war. The League, however, should be seen *not only as a possible means of preventing future wars, but much more as a great organ of the ordinary peaceful life of civilization,*[23] he held. *It must be woven into the very texture of our political system,*[24] its establishment was the Conference's *primary and basic task*[25] and *one of the great creative acts of history.*[26] *It will be,* he concluded, *the great response to the age-long cry from the human heart for 'Peace on earth, goodwill among men'.*[27]

Despite the objection of William Morris Hughes, the diminutive but persistent and politically awkward Prime Minister of Australia, that the League was a form of interfering super-state, it was agreed to forward Smuts's pamphlet to President Wilson as an expression of the British view. Meanwhile, however, both Hughes and Lloyd George were preoccupied by more immediate concerns. A Committee on Indemnity set up by Lloyd George under Hughes's chairmanship, had reported, with scant regard to facts or figures, that Germany was capable of reimbursing the total cost of the

War to the Allies; and Lloyd George's use of this report in his election campaign was raising high expectations. Smuts had warned the Prime Minister to be cautious. The Hughes Committee, with its *quite impossible recommendations on indemnities*, he wrote, *may place the Government in a very difficult position, and you may find yourself committed to much more than you desire to be.*[28] But Lloyd George, carried away or at any rate carried back into office with a huge majority on the slogan 'Full Indemnities and Punishment for the Kaiser', paid no heed to these counsels of moderation.

South Africa's Representation

Botha and Smuts arrived in Paris on 11 January 1919. Botha had come to Europe to represent his country as Prime Minister, and Smuts, as he put it, was now *only the second representative of South Africa.*[29] His prestige, however, remained second to none, thanks to his military successes, his unswerving loyalty to the Empire, his prominent role in the War Cabinet and his many services, fresh in the public mind. His liberal credentials were exceptional. President Wilson was enraptured by his League of Nations scheme and Smuts started out with high hopes. *I expect good work from this Conference*, he wrote. *It is very slow, but in the end good will come of these deliberations.*[30]

Despite the initial opposition of the American President, who thought it a subterfuge to increase Britain's voting power, all four Dominions, South Africa, Canada, Australia and New Zealand, obtained the right to an independent voice at the Conference. Smuts marvelled at the transformation of his country's status in the 17 years since 1902 when, as he wrote to Isie, he had had *to drink the cup to the bitter lees* at Vereeniging. Now, only nine years after the establishment of the

Union, *South Africa takes her place among the nations of the world*.[31] South Africa had earned that place. 140,000 South Africans had been mobilized and fought on the Western Front and against the Turks as well as in the African campaigns. 9,000 were killed, twice as many, Smuts reckoned, *as our total Boer losses in our war*,[32] and 12,000 were wounded. At the Somme in 1916, of more than 3,000 Springboks who fought in the bloody Battle of Delville Wood, only 768 came out of the wood alive.

Recognition at the Conference was important for another reason. General Hertzog was preparing to come to Paris with a deputation of Afrikaner Nationalists to agitate for secession from the Empire in the name of self-determination. Lloyd George himself would hear his claim and dismiss it on the grounds that Hertzog spoke only for the party of opposition. It was essential, however, for Smuts and Botha to consolidate their legitimacy among their own people and to demonstrate that South Africa stood to gain at Paris as a member of the Commonwealth.

Smuts was impatient at the pace of the Conference. He favoured getting to grips with the big issues straightaway and the quick conclusion of a preliminary peace; but President Wilson insisted on a comprehensive settlement and the Big Three (Wilson, Lloyd George and Clemenceau – Prime Minister Orlando of Italy playing little part) showed small sense of priority or urgency. Smuts was also pained by the speechmaking and the rhetoric of retributive justice. The inaugural Plenary Session at the Quai d'Orsay on 18 January he described as a *farce*, and he was disgusted at the opening address by *the smug Poincaré*, President Raymond Poincaré of France, the host nation. *What a poor beginning!* wrote Smuts. *Here is a world waiting for the Word, for some crumb of comfort. And we had nothing to say except punishment for war crimes.*[33] He deplored the time-wasting, squabbling and special pleading over details as the new states laboriously set forth their territorial claims. W*hether the boundary is just here or just there*, he commented, *leaves me stone cold.*[34] Overall, however, he remained sanguine. He approved Lloyd George's policy on Russia, his efforts to try and engage all sides to the civil war in peace talks and to resist renewed calls for military intervention. *Our little Prime Minister is really very good on this subject*, he commented. *I have never seen him sounder.*[35]

Smuts, Wilson and the League of Nations

For both Smuts and Wilson *the real business of this Conference*[36] was the League of Nations. Wilson had come to Paris with proposals of his own but he was captivated by Smuts's pamphlet on the League. That the League should be *the heir to this great estate* of new European nations was a phrase often on the President's lips. He found Smuts 'an extraordinary person' and thought him 'a brick'.[37]

At a Plenary Session of the Conference on 25 January it was agreed that the League would be established as 'an integral part of the Treaty of Peace'.[38] A committee was struck to draft its constitution, or Covenant, as Wilson called it. Wilson himself was chairman, Smuts and Lord Robert Cecil, author an earlier scheme for a League of Nations, were the British Empire representatives. Smuts deliberately said little, content to *have kept well in the background*[39] and let Wilson take the lead. Wilson was soon talking of the Covenant as if it were all his own work, while incorporating in it many of Smuts's proposals, often word for word. 'It is almost entirely Smuts and Phillimore combined',[40] noted Cecil. *Who minds*, Smuts commented, *so long as the work gets done?*[41] In this way, a great part of the Covenant bore Smuts's imprint, notably Articles 2 to 5 (on the Assembly and Council), Article 8 (on disarmament), Articles 12 and 13 (on international arbitration), 15 and 16 (on sanctions) and 22 (on Mandates). Wilson presented the draft Covenant to a Plenary Session of the Conference on 14 February. 'A living thing is born',[42] he declared.

Smuts held out strongly for an ethical imperative at the Conference. *We can but do what appears best, and leave the rest to God,*[43] he wrote to Alice Clark on 23 January. A week later Cecil recorded: 'He made a long elocution to me on the advantages of complete straightforwardness and honesty, and the importance of merely doing your duty and not caring about the result.' 'It was very impressive,' Cecil commented, but a colleague to whom he passed this on 'indulged in Homeric laughter'.[44]

From first to last and inevitably, as at any international conference, there were competing interests at Paris, infighting among the Delegations and jockeying for national advantage. *There is a bad spirit about,* Smuts noted, adding wryly, *mostly of course among the other fellows!*[45] He was *much haunted by the dread that this may be another Congress of Vienna,* the conference of aristocrats who after Napoleon's defeat had parcelled out Europe among the restored monarchies and formed a so-called 'Holy Alliance' to prevent further change. *For in that case,* he warned, *our League of Nations will and must become another Holy Alliance, built on fear and distrust.*[46] Not that South Africa was without special interests. The Afrikaner press was warning Botha and Smuts not to 'show themselves before the public of South Africa without German South-West Africa in their pocket'.[47]

German South-West Africa

When he devised the Mandate system, Smuts had in mind the fledgling states hatched from the former Austro-Hungarian, Russian and Ottoman Empires which the League should nurse to economic and political adulthood. He had never intended it to apply to the German colonies. These, he held, should be annexed outright, chiefly by the British Dominions. In *The League of Nations*, he dismissed the indigenous peoples of the German colonies as *barbarians, who not only cannot possibly govern themselves but to whom it would be impracticable to apply any idea of political self-determination in the European sense.*[48] On the other hand, the fifth of Wilson's Fourteen Points called for 'a free, open-minded and absolutely impartial adjustment of colonial claims'. At the first post-Armistice meeting of the Imperial War Cabinet and on several subsequent occasions, Smuts had again firmly staked South Africa's claim to German South-West Africa and his preference that Britain should annex German East Africa. This view, he said, was *very strongly felt in the Union*, which had done all the fighting in the former theatre of war and most of it in the latter. Arthur Balfour, the Foreign Secretary, observed that Smuts's demands were 'perhaps playing a little fast-and-loose with the notion of mandatory occupation',[49] and Wilson indeed protested that unless responsibility for colonial Mandates was vested in the League of Nations, the Mandate system would merely serve to enable the Allies 'to divide up the spoils'.[50]

Since long before the creation of the Union, however, Smuts and Botha had dreamed of a Greater South Africa under white rule. Smuts had pressed such claims during the War, and victory in 1918 suggested they could become a reality. A Greater South Africa should incorporate the British Crown Colony of Basutoland (now Lesotho) and the

Protectorates of Bechuanaland (now Botswana) and Swazi-land. It should stretch north at least as far as the Congo and Zambezi. It should acquire parts of Portuguese East Africa (Mozambique) by trading conquered territory in Tanganyika for the Indian Ocean littoral of Delagoa Bay and the ports of Lourenço Marques (Maputo) and Beira, so as to *give South Africa a natural frontier and round it off as a compact block of sub-tropical territory.*[51]

At the Conference, however, Wilson was proving difficult even in respect of South-West Africa. The President, Smuts wrote only half-joking to Margaret Gillett, *is entirely opposed to our annexing a little German colony here or there, which pains me deeply.*[52] Lloyd George 'chortled greatly'[53] up his sleeve at Smuts's predicament and Smuts himself appreciated the irony. To Margaret Gillett he wrote that his best argument was that most of South-West Africa consisted of the Kalahari Desert, *no good to anybody.* He was, he admitted, like the girl who pleaded that her illegitimate baby was *only a very little one!*[54]

At the end of January, the Dominions listed their demands in the presence of a sternly disapproving Wilson. Smuts put the case for South-West Africa. The Germans, he said, had ruled badly, had done little to improve the land and had all but exterminated the native Hereros. As a German base, South-West Africa would remain a dangerous neighbour to South Africa. Unlike Germany's other African possessions (the Cameroons, Togoland and Tanganyika), it was mostly desert. It could be properly developed only by South Africa with which it was *geographically one.* Botha's authority, and implicitly his own, depended on retaining the territory, and unless it was ceded, the result would be *the overthrow of General Botha and all his policy.*[55]

Hughes's uncompromising demands for German New Guinea and the Marshall Islands, bluntly conveyed in his *strident voice*,[56] met with an icy response from Wilson, who asked loftily whether Australia was 'prepared to defy the opinion of the whole civilized world'. 'That's about the size of it, Mr President,' replied Hughes. 'That puts it very well.'[57] Botha, anxious to avoid a clash with America, intervened tactfully to say that he was willing to accept a Mandate for South-West Africa.

The question now was: what *was* a Mandate and how was it to be construed? Smuts set to work on a formula (which became Article 22 of the League Covenant) under which territories Mandated by the League of Nations were classified as category 'A', 'B' or 'C' Mandates respectively according to their readiness for independence. Thus Mesopotamia (Iraq), Transjordan (Jordan) and Palestine were allocated to Britain, and Syria and Lebanon to France, as 'A' Mandates. Tanganyika became a British 'B' Mandate as did the Cameroons and Togo, divided between Britain and France. *Backward areas*, including the Pacific islands and South-West Africa, would be held by a designated Dominion, nominally as a Class C Mandate. A Class C Mandate was virtually indistinguishable from annexation save only that the Mandatory Power was required to submit an annual report to the League.

Wilson intimated to his right-hand man Colonel Edward M House his willingness to accept this face-saving formula 'if the interpretation were to come in practice from General Smuts',[58] as opposed to Hughes, whom he described as 'a pestiferous varmint'.[59] It did, and Smuts duly secured the Mandate for South-West Africa. In years to come the coveted possession would prove a mixed blessing, especially after 1924 when its German population was granted South African citizenship. This, however, lay in the future. For the present, Smuts could write to Margaret Gillett: *I look upon the mandatory system as now settled.*[60]

4
The Fight for Revision
(i): March–April 1919

Smuts enjoyed at Paris his usual rude health and spirits, invigorated by long daily walks in the Bois de Boulogne: he thought nothing of striding out for 10 miles or more; but in mid-February, after an excursion to Soissons under freezing skies in an open car to view the war-zone, he fell ill. He returned to England and was again prostrated by two successive bouts of influenza. Alice Clark, Margaret Gillett and their younger sister Hilda, a doctor, helped to nurse him back to health, but he did not fully recover for over a month and only returned to Paris on 23 March. A telegram from Paris on 10 March assured him that Lloyd George 'considers there is no need for you to return to Paris this week';[1] but what Smuts heard of developments there was disconcerting. He returned, he believed, *in the nick of time*.[2]

On arrival, he made it his business to find out quickly what had been going on and how far the 'Big Three' (Wilson, Clemenceau and Lloyd George) had committed themselves. Since the beginning of March, in order to speed up the Conference, they had been deciding matters in private and the results confirmed Smuts's worst fears. On 26 March, three days after his return to Paris, he penned a long letter to Lloyd George. As a commentary on events it is one of the most striking, though unofficial, documents of the Conference. He addressed the Prime Minister *with brutal frankness.*[3] *It won't,* he warned Lloyd George, *be pleasant reading to you.*[4] He pointed out the direction that peacemaking had taken in his absence, utterly at odds with the idealism proclaimed during the War and reiterated at the Armistice, when Lloyd George had pledged himself to uphold 'the strict principles of right'.[5] *I am seriously afraid,* wrote Smuts, *that the peace to which we are working is an impossible peace, conceived on a wrong basis: that it will not be accepted by Germany, and, even if accepted, that it will prove utterly unstable.*

To my mind, he continued, *certain points seem quite clear and elementary:*

1. *We cannot destroy Germany without destroying Europe.*
2. *We cannot save Europe without the cooperation of Germany.*

The fact is, he emphasised, *the Germans are, have been, and will continue to be the <u>dominant factor</u> on the Continent of Europe, and no permanent peace is possible which is not based on that fact.* While six weeks earlier he had held out the 1814 Congress of Vienna as a horrendous warning, he now marvelled at its good sense and moderation. After a quarter-century of war with France, the despised diplomats of the Congress had shown the wisdom to recognise *France as necessary to Europe. And yet we presume to look down upon them and their work!*

Smuts condemned the terms for a settlement with Germany

THE PRE-ARMISTICE AGREEMENT, 5 NOVEMBER 1918
In an exchange of correspondence 5–23 October 1918 between the German Chancellor and President Wilson, Germany agreed to a peace based on Wilson's Fourteen Points speech of 8 January 1918 and the principles and particulars enunciated in his subsequent speeches. On 4 November the Allies informed Wilson of their acceptance of the same terms, subject to a proviso covering Point 2 (freedom of the seas) and the Points relating to the 'restoration' of invaded territory. On 5 November, the US Secretary of State, Robert Lansing, sent the following note (known as the Lansing Note or Pre-Armistice Agreement) to the Swiss Minister in Washington (representing German interests in the USA) for transmission to Berlin...

'The President is now in receipt of a memorandum of observations by the allied Governments on this correspondence which is as follows:

The allied Governments have given careful consideration to the correspondence which has passed between the President of the United States and the German Government. Subject to the qualifications which follow, they declare their willingness to make peace with the Government of Germany on the terms of peace laid down in the President's address to Congress of January, 1918, and the principles of settlement enunciated in his subsequent addresses.

They must point out, however, that Clause 2, relating to what is usually described as the freedom of the seas, is open to various interpretations, some of which they could not accept. They must,

which the Big Three had more or less agreed amongst themselves as unjust, unnecessary and unworkable. How could Germany, wracked by forces of dissent from Left and Right, keep internal order with an army restricted to 100,000? Britain could barely cope with that number in *poor unarmed Ireland*. The territorial provisions left him aghast: the proposed transfer to Poland of the port of Danzig, *an ancient German town with a German population*, and of West Prussia (to form the Polish Corridor to the sea), *together with some millions of Germans*; the projected cession of the Saarland to France and therefore, reserve to themselves complete freedom on this subject when they enter the peace negotiations.

Further, in the conditions of peace, laid down in his address to Congress of Jan. 8, 1918, the President declared that invaded territories must be restored as well as evacuated and freed. The allied Governments feel that no doubt ought to be allowed to exist as to what this provision implies. By it they understand that compensation will be made by Germany for all damage done to the civilian population of the Allies and their property by the aggression of Germany by land, by sea and from the air.

I am instructed by the President to say that he is in agreement with the interpretation of the last paragraph of the memorandum above quoted. I am further instructed by the President to request you to notify the German Government that Marshal Foch has been authorized by the Government of the United States and the allied Governments to receive properly accredited representatives of the German Government and to communicate to them terms of an armistice ...'

On receipt of this note, the German Government immediately sent representatives to Marshal Ferdinand Foch. The Armistice was signed on 11 November.

At a meeting of the British Empire Delegation on 1 June 1919, Smuts challenged *any lawyer to go through the correspondence with the Germans before the Armistice and then to say that the Allies were not bound to make a peace on Wilson's terms and on the basis of his speeches.*

the detachment from Germany of all her territory west of the Rhine. *I am simply amazed at all this*, he exclaimed. *Are we in our sober senses, or suffering from shellshock? What has become of Wilson's Fourteen Points, or of your repeated declarations against the humiliation and dismemberment of Germany?* All these amputations of German territory he considered *most dangerous, and indeed fatal from the point of view of securing present and future peace. If the Germans are like the rest of us*, he observed, *they simply will not accept such terms.*

Smuts warned against attempting to set up the new nation-states neighbouring Germany at Germany's expense and against her will: *In trying to break Germany in order to create and territorially satisfy these smaller States, we are labouring at a task which is bound to fail*. The new States should be founded not in the teeth of German resistance but with active German help. *The fact is*, he argued, *neither Poland nor Bohemia* [Czechoslovakia] *will be politically possible without German goodwill and assistance. They ought to be established on a basis which will secure German cooperation in their future success*. Germany *ought not to be despoiled and treated as an international pariah*, he maintained. *Instead of dismembering and destroying Germany, she ought in a measure to be taken into the scope of our policy, and be made responsible for part of the burden which is clearly too heavy for us to bear* in *the defence and assistance of central Europe*. Britain lacked the manpower and capacity to police Central Europe, and *without German goodwill, neither Poland nor Bohemia will show any stable vitality*. They would *become simply problems and burdens for the future politics of Europe*. Thus Danzig should not be torn from Germany in order to give Poland the access to the Baltic promised in the Fourteen Points; instead Poland should be granted transit rights across German territory.

Smuts's arguments were prudent and prophetic: no settlement could last without genuine German support. *Even at this late hour*, he besought the Prime Minister, *I would urge that we revise our attitude towards Germany*. While Germany should *pay heavily* to make good the physical destruction she had inflicted, she should also be required to take on responsibility *for the defence and assistance of Central Europe* and should *join the League of Nations from the beginning*. Smuts believed that *her appeasement now* would make Germany a bulwark against Bolshevism. He ended by invoking what he always cherished as the shining example of international statesmanship: the *political magnanimity* shown by Campbell-Bannerman to South Africa after the Boer War, which had brought such rich rewards.

Smuts was frank and direct in his admonitions. *I note the stand you have made against some of these things, but,* he warned, *that is not enough. We shall be judged, not by our protests, but by our acts.* Unless the peace was recast in a wholly different spirit, *the statesmen connected with it will return to their countries broken, discredited men.*[6]

That Smuts could write a letter of such candour to the Prime Minister shows the measure of the man and his standing. He believed he had made an impression on Lloyd George: *I think the effect has been very great.*[7] How deep that impression really was and how lasting its effect was another matter. True, Lloyd George called him in for a man-to-man discussion. Smuts *talked over the whole matter with the Prime Minister, who,* he claimed, *largely agrees with me,* though, as he rightly added, *one never knows the orbits of minds like his.*[8] On the very day he received Smuts's letter, Lloyd George raised it in discussion with Clemenceau and Wilson. The fact was that much

> My experience in South Africa has made me a firm believer in political magnanimity, and your and Campbell-Bannerman's great record still remains not only the noblest, but also the most successful, page in recent British statesmanship. On the other hand, I fear, I greatly fear our present panic policy towards Germany will bring failure on this Conference, and spell ruin for Europe.
>
> J C SMUTS TO LLOYD GEORGE, 26 MARCH 1919

of it echoed his own second thoughts as expressed in his Fontainebleau Memorandum. This document, aimed chiefly at French policy, called for a moderate peace which a German Government could sign in good faith.

Smuts's timely letter thus provided Lloyd George with ammunition in his current revisionist mood. The Prime Minister stressed Smuts' objections to ceding Danzig to Poland. This, said Lloyd George, citing the letter, was 'the opposite of statesmanlike',[9] as was the proposed transfer to Poland of two million Germans. The terms contemplated amounted to 'a very harsh peace,' he said. 'Put at their lowest, our terms will be such that no civilized nation has ever had to accept anything like them.'[10] Lloyd George preferred to make Danzig a Free City under League of Nations sovereignty. He cited Smuts's argument that Poland could not thrive without German goodwill. This meeting of the Big Three ended with Lloyd George reading aloud Smuts's letter and its reminder that, whatever the terms, Germany would remain *the dominant factor* in Europe. Clemenceau and Wilson were less impressed than he expected, however, and Clemenceau commented that he hoped Smuts was not speaking as a friend of Germany.

Mission to Central Europe

I am giving a helping hand with the most important points in the Peace Treaty,[11] Smuts wrote to Margaret Gillett. But *as usual*, he reflected of Lloyd George, *when I am pressing very hard on his conscience, he wants to send me on some distant mission.*[12] And indeed, Lloyd George now appointed Smuts to head an Allied Mission to Budapest. Central and Eastern Europe were in turmoil. In January Smuts had noted that *in eastern Europe about a dozen little wars are being waged.*[13]

They were still raging in March; and Smuts feared that, as long as the Allies refused to lift the blockade, peoples made desperate by chaos and starvation would fall prey to Bolshevism. On 21 March the liberal government of Count Mihály Károlyi, foolishly snubbed by the Big Three, was ousted by a Communist revolution in Budapest. Hungary became a Soviet Republic under Bela Kun, an associate of Lenin. There was consternation in Paris and fears of similar outbreaks in Germany and Austria. The Romanians used it as an excuse to cross the Armistice line and advance into Hungary. The ostensible purpose of Smuts's mission was to reassert the authority of the Allies and to hold the ring between Hungary and Romania.

When Kun signalled his willingness to receive an Allied Mission, Lloyd George was keen to respond. 'Let us not act towards Hungary as we did in the case of Russia,' he told Wilson and Clemenceau. 'One Russia is enough for us.'[14] He proposed Smuts as Head of Mission. The President 'nodded vigorously and said that he was just the man',[15] though Smuts's nomination 'did not altogether commend itself to M. Clemenceau'.[16] 'A curious business,' Sir Henry Wilson, Chief of the Imperial General Staff, wrote in his diary. 'A Welshman sends a Dutchman to tell a Hungarian not to fight a Rumanian.'[17]

Smuts saw in his mission a possible opportunity to negotiate with Kun as an intermediary for Lenin, perhaps even for a meeting in Budapest with the Russian Bolshevik leaders themselves, he suggested to Lloyd George, which might *lead to peace with Russia and thus round off the work of this Peace Conference.*[18] *Miracles do happen*, he wrote to Margaret Gillett, *I have seen several in my short life.*[19] This miracle did not happen.

Smuts and his party of Allied officials, who included Harold Nicolson of the Foreign Office, left Paris by the night express for Vienna on 1 April. Via Switzerland, the train crossed Austria, the people there visibly drawn and pinched in consequence of the blockade. At Vienna the British Military Attaché had laid on a sumptuous luncheon at Sacher's restaurant. Smuts was furious. He angrily reprimanded the attaché for *a gross error in taste*[20] and henceforth on his orders the Mission lived off its own army rations. Reaching Budapest by special train on 4 April, Smuts declined the hotel accommodation offered by Bela Kun and insisted that negotiations take place on the train at the railway station, where he remained throughout the Mission, scrupulous to give no appearance of official recognition to Kun's regime.

> 'Smuts is silent, dignified, reserved. A huge luncheon at Sacher's, which cost 1200 kronen. Smuts is furious. He ticks Cunninghame off sharply. He calls it a *gross error in taste*. He decrees that from now on we shall feed only upon our own army rations and not take anything from these starving countries. His eyes when angry are like steel rods. But it was a good luncheon all the same.'
>
> HAROLD NICOLSON, DIARY, 3 APRIL 1919, ON J C SMUTS'S ARRIVAL IN VIENNA EN ROUTE FOR BUDAPEST

Smuts informed Kun of the Allied demand that Hungarian troops withdraw to the Armistice line, which they had in turn overrun in order to repel the invading Romanians. Kun said no Hungarian government could enforce such a directive, but suggested the question of frontiers between Hungary and her neighbours should be determined at a special conference under Smuts's direction. He argued that questions of food and the economy were more urgent than frontier disputes and that some sort of Danubian economic federation was essential.

Smuts was sympathetic to these proposals. He recommended talks in Paris to fix Hungary's boundaries in a preliminary treaty and advised that the Allies should send food supplies to Central Europe immediately. However, he also saw that Kun's regime would not last, and obtained leave to terminate the Mission. Unaware of this, Kun tried to haggle, but Smuts cut him short by ordering the train to leave on the appointed hour, leaving the astonished Hungarians standing speechless on the platform. 'We glide out into the night,' wrote Nicolson, 'retaining on the retinas of our eyes the picture of four bewildered faces.' [21]

BELA KUN (1886–1938)
A left-wing journalist, Kun fought for Austria-Hungary in the First World War. Taken prisoner by the Russians in 1916, he became a Communist and friend of Lenin. He headed the short-lived Communist regime in Hungary March to August 1919, then fled to Russia, where he became a member of the Comintern. He was executed in one of Stalin's purges in 1938.

The Mission returned via Prague, where at Lloyd George's request Smuts raised with Tomáš Masaryk, President of Czechoslovakia, the wisdom of extending the new state's southern boundaries at Hungary's expense. *With some millions of Germans already included* in the Sudetenland to the north, as Smuts reported presciently, the incorporation of half a million Hungarians in the south *would be a very serious matter for the young State, besides the grave violation of the principle of nationality involved.*[22] Masaryk appeared to agree, but the warning was ignored. Smuts and Masaryk also discussed economic cooperation between the states of the former Austro-Hungarian Empire before Smuts left for Vienna where he held similar talks with the Austrian Finance Minister, Josef Schumpeter, and also found time to greet his old wartime acquaintance, Count von Mensdorff. He was back in Paris on 9 April and his report was with Lloyd George within an hour of his arrival.

The Times, vehemently anti-Bolshevik, dismissed his Mission as a 'wasted journey'.[23] It is true that Smuts's hopes were not realised. Yet it showed him at his best: imaginative, positive, constructive. *Although I did not succeed in my ostensible mission to Hungary*, he wrote, *I think I have won those people over to our side and kept them away from Russia.*[24] He returned profoundly affected by what he had seen of collapse and demoralization in the former Austria-Hungary – *the pitiful plight of Central Europe*, commenting to Margaret Gillett that n*othing so burns up every particle of self as the sights I have passed through during the last week.*[25] *Never in my life*, he wrote to Alice Clark, *have I seen such a load of despair on people's minds*; such human realities, he felt, should *cure us of our smallness and narrowness and forgive our wild hankerings after indemnities and queer efforts to press blood out of the stones.*[26]

The morning after his return to Paris he breakfasted with Lloyd George and gave him a first-hand account of conditions in Vienna, *a world completely gone to pieces.*[27] His own adjutant, he said, had seen a British soldier distributing buns to children almost lynched by a mob of starving urchins. A week later Lloyd George retailed this vivid episode in a speech to the House of Commons. And yet the Prime Minister was as set on squeezing indemnities from these ruined states as from Germany, even though, as Smuts objected, the Allies would rather need *to advance them money to live.*[28] Smuts was convinced that Austria-Hungary should remain a single economic unit as under the Habsburgs, and that the frontiers of the successor states should not form trade barriers between them. He argued for a sub-conference in Paris at which the successor states should be represented to discuss a Danubian economic federation and an international loan to set it in motion, and *where the genuine preliminaries of peace in Central Europe could be established.*[29]

He raised these concerns again as a member of the so-called Supreme Economic Council, a non-executive body set up to advise on the provision of food, finance, shipping and raw materials in Europe. At a meeting on 23 April, he expounded John Maynard Keynes's ideas for an international credit loan to Europe, especially to the Danubian states. But this scheme, which pre-figured the post-Second World War Marshall Plan, was ahead of its time. The Americans refused to advance further loans in order, as they saw it, to finance reparation provisions of which they disapproved, when they were themselves already owed huge sums by the Allies. The Supreme Economic Council played no part in drawing up the economic clauses of the Treaty and Smuts's appeals fell on deaf ears. The Council was *another talking shop which does nothing,* he wrote to Alice Clark. *Will the Lord never rid us of these debating societies? Oh for an ounce of action.*[30]

Reparations and Reputations

Of all the problems facing the Peace Conference, reparations from Germany were the most intractable and time-consuming. Smuts always took a moderate line on this. He approved, as fair and within Germany's capacity, the memorandum which Keynes submitted at the time of the Armistice, recommending a total of some £2 billion in the gold values of 1914. He had tried to dissuade Lloyd George from his electoral pledges to exact far more. In his letter of 26 March 1919, he again urged him to *look at the matter from a large point of view, and not ask the impossible.*[31] The Prime Minister, however, was aiming at a figure, now in the public domain, of at least £10 billion.

Lloyd George's latest stratagem to maximise Britain's share, which he now pressed on Wilson, was a demand that Germany bear the cost of state pensions for Britain's injured servicemen and the separation allowances payable to dependants of men on active service. Under the Pre-Armistice Agreement of 5 November 1918, Germany had accepted liability 'for all damage done to the civilian population of the Allies and their property' – a formula devised by Lloyd George himself. Military pensions and separation allowances did not on the face of it come within this definition. Yet without these items Britain's share of reparations would be meagre compared to those of France and Belgium. The President, however, rejected Lloyd George's latest claims as incompatible with the Pre-Armistice Agreement. At Lloyd George's behest, Lord Sumner, a distinguished Law Lord and principal British Delegate on reparations, endeavoured to persuade the Americans of Germany's liability for these costs. A soldier, he maintained, was 'simply a civilian called to arms. His uniform makes no difference'. Wilson dismissed this as 'very legalistic'.[32]

Lloyd George was ever resourceful. Mindful of Wilson's admiration for Smuts and of Smuts's influence on Wilson in the matter of colonial Mandates, he turned to Smuts. Hence it was that late on Sunday 30 March, two days before he left for Budapest, Smuts had found himself drafting a legal opinion along the desired lines. He worked into the early hours. *The PM wanted my opinion to show to Wilson,* he wrote to Margaret Gillett, *as he says Wilson will not listen to the English lawyer but will pay attention to what I say. It is a farcical world*.[33] Of the resulting opinion which Lloyd George handed to Wilson the next morning, W K Hancock, Smuts's official biographer, writes: 'it has done more damage to his reputation than any other document that he ever produced in his whole life'.[34] Smuts's argument was the same as Sumner's: *What was or is spent on the citizen before he became a soldier or after he has ceased to be a soldier, or at any time on his family, represents compensation for damage done to civilians and must be made good by the German Government.* It followed that *this includes all war pensions and separation allowances.*[35]

It was this document that persuaded Wilson, against the advice of his own lawyers; he was, he said, 'very much impressed'.[36] The President 'admires Smuts extravagantly,'[37] his Secretary of State noted sardonically. Wilson agreed it was illogical to distinguish pensions and separation allowances from any other item of war expenditure, but he felt wounded combatants and servicemen's dependents were objects of particular compassion – 'I don't give a damn for logic!'[38] he exclaimed – and should in common justice be a charge on reparations. He also wanted to help the British Prime Minister out of a difficulty. Lloyd George had pledged to 'make Germany pay' and made out that his political survival depended on the inclusion of these items. Both Smuts and Wilson thought it fair that Britain, as the highest spender of the War, should receive a decent share of reparations, and both supposed at the time that the contentious items would merely increase Britain's allocation of a finite total, not that they would inflate and indeed triple the amount eventually demanded.

For Keynes, however, Wilson's decision on pensions marked 'the most decisive moment in the disintegration of the President's moral position',[39] and he was to heap scorn and execration on him for it in *The Economic Consequences of the Peace*. And because Smuts produced the opinion that induced Wilson's change of mind, Smuts's opinion too became the butt of criticism from which it has never recovered. Keynes would denounce it as 'flimsy and worthless', 'a masterpiece of the sophist's art' and 'little more than a trick'.[40] This was unjust and overdrawn. The case was at the very least arguable. Wilson's own legal adviser, John Foster Dulles, while coming to an opposite conclusion, agreed that it was a moot point. Smuts himself stood by his opinion – he was after all a lawyer and Keynes was not.[41] Keynes's attacks were seized on in South Africa by Hertzog and his Nationalists, for whom any excuse was good enough to vilify 'Slim Jannie'. But even Keynes regretted the irony that Smuts of all men should take the blame.

5

The Fight for Revision (ii): May 1919

On his return from Budapest, Smuts still had hopes of a moderate peace. Lloyd George was achieving some measure of success – at a price. He and Wilson had forced Clemenceau to back down on the separation from Germany of the left bank of the Rhine; but in return the Prime Minister had reluctantly acquiesced in a 15-year Allied military occupation of the Rhineland (a period which could be extended), and he and Wilson had offered Clemenceau in addition a guarantee of Anglo-American intervention in the event of future German aggression.

Smuts, who opposed any occupation of Germany, urged the Prime Minister to resist any but the shortest. He also encouraged him to resist the mounting clamour at Westminster for heavy reparations. Lloyd George had all along been out for all he could get from Germany, but he appealed, somewhat disingenuously, for Smuts's understanding of the political pressures on him. He was also under attack from within the Empire Delegation. Hughes, wholly dissatisfied on reparations, threatened to publicise his dissent. Smuts wrote sympathetically to Lloyd George but urged him to *take the responsibility and face the music, whatever Parliaments or peoples may say.*[1]

The Big Three were now anxious to finalise the Treaty. Their time-table was badly awry. The German Plenipotentiaries had presented themselves on demand at Versailles at the end of April and were waiting there to receive the terms. Thus it was that Smuts found himself *snowed under with work* as he poured over a mass of incoming reports from the various Conference Commissions. *I have to wade through numerous intricate and verbose reports on all sorts of uninteresting subjects*, he wrote. *Uninteresting to me*, he added significantly, *but not to the enemy under the harrow, and there is the rub.*[2] It was originally assumed these reports, namely detailed recommendations for the individual chapters of the Treaty, would be thrashed out in discussion, revised, refined and amended by the Allies before being presented to the Germans for face-to-face negotiation. It now turned out, such had been the lack of basic organising principles from the start and so many were the weeks that had been spent on secondary matters, that these disparate reports, drawn up as statements of maximum demands, were now hurriedly collated without adequate coordination or review and incorporated unaltered as the terms of the draft Treaty. The result was a mish-mash of ill-assorted and incongruous provisions, good and bad. One of many bad clauses stipulated the surrender of nearly 900 alleged war criminals. Smuts and Botha argued for a select shortlist of the worst suspects. Only after the Treaty had been ratified a year later was this agreed.

On the very eve of its presentation to the Germans, Smuts, like most of his colleagues, still had no complete copy of the draft Treaty, which was with the printers. There was no opportunity for the British Delegation to read it and discuss it in full beforehand. From what he knew of it already however – and Smuts knew more than most – he was dismayed. *I am much troubled over our peace terms*, he wrote to Alice Clark. *I consider them bad. And wrong.*[4] After consulting Keynes, he now concluded that the reparation chapter was *impossible*,[5] and the Treaty as a whole disastrous, vicious in content and even in tone. Botha particularly deplored its many gratuitous 'pinpricks' and Smuts agreed. It was shot through with *a petty, small spirit*, he complained. *And of all shortcomings that is the worst.*[6] *I wish fifty per cent of this Peace Treaty could be scrapped*,[7] he wrote to Margaret Gillett.

> I am getting more and more uneasy and unhappy over the terms of peace. I think they are wrong. They will either not be accepted or if accepted they will not be carried out. They will leave a trail of anarchy, ruin and bitterness in their wake for another generation ... And all through our own unwisdom. What shall I do?
>
> **J C SMUTS TO MARGARET GILLETT, 2 MAY 1919**[3]

He decided once more to beard the Prime Minister, who he sensed *has been avoiding me recently.*[8] Less than 48 hours remained before the handover. Accordingly, on 5 May he wrote urgently to Lloyd George. He pressed for the terms to be amended, *if possible, before the document is published or handed to the Germans.* His letter took the form of a terse recapitulation of his objections, set out under half a dozen heads corresponding to the main chapters of the Treaty. The clauses on Danzig and the Saar, he wrote, *go too far.* The military restrictions *leave Germany an army far too small for her requirements.* The reparations chapter was *too drastic.* The *punishment clauses could not honourably be accepted by any Government.* The international controls to be imposed on Germany's rivers and railways were *hopelessly one-sided*. For Smuts, however, *the most shocking of all* were *the occupation provisions. That France can remain for fifteen years at least in occupation of the left bank of the Rhine*, he wrote, *must shock every decent conscience.*[9]

Smuts also tried another approach – that of political pressure. Lloyd George had offered Clemenceau, on behalf of Britain and the Empire, a military guarantee against future German aggression. Smuts now drafted a letter to Lloyd George, which Botha signed, warning the Prime Minister against including South Africa in the guarantee. If Smuts supposed, however, that this would deter such a wily operator as Lloyd George, he was much mistaken. The Prime Minister, whose own good faith in the matter was dubious, simply amended the guarantee to read that it would not be binding on the Dominions until ratified by them. Constitutionally speaking, it was true that by this side-wind Smuts had obtained a concession of the utmost significance for South Africa: formal recognition that the Dominions were no longer bound by Britain's treaty obligations and were henceforth free to make their own choices as independent states. But Smuts's démarche failed in its immediate object: to shift Lloyd George on the German Treaty.

No changes were made to the terms, now still being rushed into print for the hand-over ceremony on 7 May. That morning, after a sleepless night, Smuts rose early. Roaming the empty boulevards, he encountered Herbert Hoover, the American Director-General of Allied Relief, who, like Smuts, had constantly urged the lifting of the blockade. 'Within a few blocks,' Hoover recalled, 'I met General Smuts and John Maynard Keynes ... We seemed to have come together by some sort of telepathy. It flashed into all our minds why each was walking about at that time of morning.' [10] On returning to his hotel, Smuts wrote sardonically to Alice Clark, *I am going in a frock-coat and top hat to Versailles just now to join in the exhilarating ceremony of handing the Boche our terms.*[11]

Accordingly, that afternoon, on *a most beautiful spring day*, Smuts was present in the Trianon Palace Hotel at Versailles to see Count Ulrich von Brockdorff-Rantzau, Foreign Minister and head of the German Delegation, take formal delivery of the draft Treaty. The scene, stage-managed by the French, seemed to Smuts *to have been conceived more in a spirit of making war than of making peace.*[13] Under the gaze of Representatives of 27 Allied and Associated nations, Brockdorff-Rantzau, stiff and ill-at-ease, felt himself to be in the dock. To the indignation of Wilson and Lloyd George, he delivered, seated, a vehement speech of protest. Lloyd George was so angry 'he felt he could get up and hit' Brockdorff-Rantzau. He said it had made him 'more angry than any incident of the war'.[14] Smuts, however, listened closely to what Brockdorff-Rantzau said. He heard his pointed reminder that Wilson's Fourteen Points were binding on both sides and constituted the legal framework to which the peace must conform. Few others had time for Brockdorff-Rantzau's protestations, however, for his manner alienated sympathy. Smuts was disconsolate. He would sit with Keynes in the evenings, he informed Margaret Gillett, *and we rail against the world and the coming flood. And I tell him that*

> **Behind the petty stage on which we pose and strut and play-act at making history there looms the dark Figure which is quietly moving the pieces of world history.**
> J C SMUTS, 7 MAY 1919, THE DAY OF THE HANDING OVER TO THE GERMANS OF THE DRAFT TERMS[12]

this is the time for the Griqua prayer[15] that the Lord should come down to earth himself and not send his Son, as it was no time for children.

This mood of passivity did not last. The last three weeks of May, during which the Germans submitted a succession of detailed comments on the draft Treaty, mark the third phase of Smuts's active intervention at the Conference. *The Peace Treaty is becoming more and more an abomination to me*, he wrote on 14 May. The same day he penned another solemn letter of warning, *a very frank memorandum*, as he called it. One copy he addressed to Lloyd George, the other to Wilson, though without informing either that he had written to the other. *It may be too late*, he wrote to Margaret Gillett, *but at any rate I must deal faithfully with them and who knows whether even at this twelfth hour they may be constrained to listen.*[16]

The more I have studied the Peace Treaty as a whole, his latest letter to Lloyd George began, *the more I dislike it.* Smuts appealed for *drastic revision.* As before, his objections were as much practical as legal or ethical. The terms, he repeated, were inconsistent and contradictory. *The combined effect of the territorial and reparation clauses*, he wrote, *is to make it practically impossible for Germany to carry out the provisions of the treaty.* To subject *East and West blocks of Germans* to the rule of *their historic enemies*, Poland and France, was to court disaster. The transfer of mainly German-populated areas to Poland, the occupation of the Rhineland *under an undefined regime of martial law* for a period potentially *even beyond the already far too long period of fifteen years* – all this was storing up untold trouble. The occupation was likely to prove inflammatory and Lloyd George's guarantee to France *may at any time bring the British Empire also into the fire.*

Under this Treaty, wrote Smuts, *Europe will know no peace. I am grieved beyond words that such should be the result of our statesmanship*. It was, he admitted, awkward to defend the German case in Paris, with the glaring evidence close at hand of the destruction wantonly wreaked in *devastated France. But now that the Germans can state their own case*, he begged Lloyd George and Wilson to allow them a fair hearing and not *to waive aside objections which will be urged by the Germans* and which, in his view, *will be supported by the good sense and conscience of most moderate people*. He appealed to the judgment and authority of the two world leaders: *I pray you will use your unrivalled power and influence to make the final treaty a more moderate and reasonable document*.[17]

But neither Lloyd George nor Wilson was in a mood to listen. *The Prime Minister*, Smuts reported, *is definitely against me now*.[18] He turned to Wilson, following up his letter with a personal request to see the President *at an early date* in order to raise with him *some matters of considerable urgency*.[19] Wilson deputed House to see him, and in a *long and very earnest talk*[20] Smuts made the strongest representations. Unless the Treaty was altered, he told House, he for one would *refuse* his *signature* to what was a *negation of Wilsonism*.[21] Wilson himself was superficially receptive, replying with 'unaffected thanks for your letter', for which 'no apology was needed'. The President, however, had dug in his heels. While agreeing that the Treaty was 'undoubtedly very severe indeed', he did not think it 'unjust in the circumstances', given 'the very great offence against civilization which the German state committed' and the need to make it clear 'once for all that such things can lead only to the most severe punishment'.[22]

Smuts's disappointment was profound. Lloyd George, *our mercurial, tricky Prime Minister*, he learned, *is very angry with me.*[23] As for the President, *I get no support from Wilson. I do not even know whether he really agrees with me. He thinks the Germans deserve a hard peace. I think the world deserves a good peace.*[24] *My own attempts to get Wilson's support have so far failed.*[25] No, he wrote to Henry Gillett on 20 May, *the so-called Peace Treaty shows little sign of my work. It is a bad and dangerous piece of work, largely born of fear and revenge, and it will not stand.*[26] On the same day, he described it to Cecil as *worse than the Treaty of Vienna, and a terrible outcome of all our professions.*[27] To Margaret Gillett he portrayed himself as a helpless and horrified spectator, watching the unfolding of *a tragedy of almost infinite dimensions, the poignancy of which is often more than one can bear.*[28] The peacemakers had failed lamentably. *I am bitterly disappointed in both Wilson and Lloyd George*, he wrote to Isie, *who are smaller men than I should ever have thought.*[29] *Wilson*, he concluded sadly, *is not really a great man.* He had abandoned the cause. *House told me that Wilson thought more of my opinion than of that of any other person on the British Delegation. That must be the reason why he is now avoiding me, when I say that this great monument is not a work of brass but of sand.*[30]

Rebuffed by Wilson and Lloyd George, Smuts keenly felt his impotence and isolation. He regretted he had not taken up Lloyd George's wartime suggestion that he stand for Parliament, for he had no political platform in Britain and was barred by confidentiality from publicising his views. On 19 May he wrote, *I made a mistake in 1917 when I did not plunge right into British politics ... For I am now only the second representative of South Africa. The terrible thing is that I dare not say in public what I really feel and what is really going on.* With no resource but his own conscience and the passionate strength of his convictions, he agonized as to what he should do. He soon made up his mind. He would carry on the fight. *I don't mean to give in so easily, and have fired off some shots which I hope will hit somebody hard.*[31]

While Smuts's repeated efforts to revise the draft Treaty ultimately failed to sway Lloyd George and Wilson they won considerable support in the American and British Delegations, to whom he circulated copies of his letters. James Headlam-Morley of the Foreign Office wrote to Smuts, 'I hope you will allow me to say how glad I am that someone has said what many are thinking ... The Treaty in its present form is indefensible and cannot in fact be carried out.'[32]

On 20 May, Smuts wrote to Isie to say that unless important revisions were made he would not sign the Treaty. It was a *terrible document.* He was *troubled in my conscience about putting my name to such a document.* He agreed with Wilson that *the Germans behaved disgracefully in the war and deserve a hard peace. But that is no reason why the world must be thrust into ruin.* Germany was being treated *as we would not treat a kaffir nation,* he wrote. *I have already protested against this, and I shall, if necessary, go further in my resistance. My children must never be ashamed of their father's signature.* If, as he believed, the Germans refused to sign and in consequence the blockade was continued, *I shall fight against this whatever the cost.*[33] He considered leading a personal campaign for Treaty revision in England and America and to that end he was prepared to resign from Botha's government. *Come weal come woe,* he wrote in a further letter to Isie that day, *we shall try to stand faithfully by what is best and highest in our view of life, and leave the rest in God's hands.*[34] Writing the same day to Henry Gillett (Arthur's cousin), he indicated the ultimate object of his opposition to the Treaty: *Behind it and undermining it we must build up a peace of understanding and human fellowship.*[35]

Meanwhile he learned that his stance was *causing some perturbation*[36] to Lloyd George. He was invited to discuss his concerns with Balfour, whom he found startlingly ignorant of much in the Treaty, though, as Smuts gently reminded him, as Foreign Secretary he was constitutionally responsible for it. Two days later, on 22 May, he was summoned by Lloyd George himself, to whom, as to Balfour, he spoke *very seriously.*[37] The Prime Minister asked him to submit his objections in writing yet again.

Accordingly, later the same day, Smuts addressed a further memorandum to the Prime Minister. Recapitulating the points he had already made, he stressed the futility of a *Diktat*, a settlement unilaterally imposed by the Allies, and the need for a peace which the Germans themselves would see as fair. *For the sake of the future*, he warned prophetically, *they should not merely be made to sign at the point of the bayonet, so to speak. The Treaty should not be capable of moral repudiation by the German people hereafter.* Hence the Allies *should as far as possible carry the German delegates with us* and *we should listen to what they have to say.*[38]

Smuts had put his finger on the Treaty's most basic and in retrospect most glaring flaw. The Peace Conference was inchoate. It never evolved, as originally intended and in the normal manner of a peace conference, into a Congress at which both sides negotiated face to face. All these months the Allies had been engrossed in the tortuous business of reaching agreement, not with the enemy, but among themselves. The time had now come, Smuts insisted, to talk to the Germans: *It will be necessary to meet them in oral discussion*. Once the Germans had submitted their final written counter-proposals, he suggested, *a small committee of minor delegates*, three in number, representing the British Empire, France and the United States, should enter into direct discussion with them on *the Treaty as a whole* and report back to the Big Three. In this way, the Treaty would be purged of *all appearance of one-sidedness and unnecessary dictation*, and its *moral authority* would be *all the greater and more binding on that account*.[39] Few more obvious or sensible comments have been made on the Paris Peace Conference. Yet this fundamental and wholly indispensable precondition of peace was no longer seriously entertained. The original objective of a Congress had long since faded from view.

It is hard not to believe that Smuts had himself in mind as one of the three *minor delegates*, though he denied it – *for I disagree with too much in the Treaty*.[40] But in any event his plea for direct talks was rejected. Botha raised it again two days later on 24 May, Smuts's 49th birthday, at a small celebratory dinner which Botha arranged, attended by Cecil, Milner, Hoover and Lloyd George himself. Smuts had already aired his latest idea to Cecil. 'I sympathized warmly,'[41] Cecil recorded, noting that 'there was some suggestion of discussing things unofficially with the Germans.' Lloyd George, however, 'seemed averse to any such plan, saying that it would be very dangerous'.[42]

The Prime Minister thus expressly ruled out negotiation with the Germans. Negotiation between the Allies had been bad enough. For four long months the Conference had dragged itself out in continuous argument on the contentious issues – and all the main issues were necessarily contentious. More than once the Conference had come close to breakdown. The Italians quitted Paris and returned to Rome for two weeks of protest. The Japanese threatened to leave. Wilson himself had prepared to return home. Clemenceau had stalked out of a meeting with Wilson, and Wilson had intervened physically when a furious Lloyd George and Clemenceau flew at each other's throats. Lloyd George had told Wilson that unless his pledges on reparations were met in full, 'I might as well go home'.[43] The resulting document was a patchwork quilt of unhappy compromises, reached only after interminable discussion and heart-searching. Only by dint of patience, persuasion and perseverance was agreement reached at all. In these circumstances, the Big Three no longer contemplated talking to the Germans. It would have meant revisiting decisions hammered out after weeks, sometimes months, of wrangling. Renegotiation would have torn the Treaty apart.

To explain is not to excuse. Smuts's objections were wise, far-sighted and accurate. *We in Paris are sowing the dragon's teeth*,[44] he wrote to Margaret Gillett. The failure to talk to the Germans, perhaps the most extraordinary, certainly the most lamentable feature of the entire Conference, inevitably turned the Treaty into a *Diktat*. But even supposing that Lloyd George had favoured Smuts's proposal, Smuts was now the last man he would have chosen to negotiate. Smuts had become a thorn in his side. Relations between them were at a nadir. As when he sent Smuts to Budapest, Lloyd George now seemed keen to staunch, at least for the moment, his unwelcome flow of criticisms of the German Treaty.

He now called on Smuts to join the Commission on Austrian Reparations. Lord Sumner, Lloyd George's hard-line advocate on German reparations, was also his principal spokesman on this Commission. Perhaps Lloyd George thought Smuts might exert a moderating influence on Sumner, though this seems unlikely for Lloyd George was as set on making large demands from Germany's ex-allies as from Germany herself and in Smuts's words, *intended to wring blood out of poor Austria and the other States carved out of that old Empire.*[45] Perhaps he sought to provoke a refusal from Smuts that would discredit him in the eyes of his colleagues. At any rate Smuts, in what he ironically called *an amusing passage with the Prime Minister,*[46] refused his request point blank. He would take no part, he told Lloyd George, in seeking reparations from *a broken, bankrupt, economically impossible State like Austria* or generally from *the dead and dismembered Austro-Hungarian Empire.*[47]

Smuts's impressions, fresh from his mission to Budapest, of civilian sufferings in Central Europe were reinforced by a letter from Hilda Clark. Currently in Vienna herself on a Quaker relief mission, she wrote to Smuts enclosing photographs of starving children, from which, as Smuts wrote to Isie, *you can see their dreadful condition clearly.*[48] Smuts would have nothing to do with a policy which, he informed Lloyd George, *could only lead to the most mischievous results,* and his letter of refusal was uncompromising. *I am,* he wrote, *against payment of all reparation by these countries.*[49]

Lloyd George replied immediately and angrily. Did Smuts intend that Britain and South Africa should be encumbered with a crushing burden of war debt for the next 30 or 40 years, while states they had liberated, and enemy states, Austria and Hungary, got off scot-free? He did not see how he could justify such a policy to Parliament.

Smuts was unimpressed. Replying next day, he repeated that any attempt to impose reparations on the former Austria-Hungary would be disastrous and would drive *all afflicted*

Central Europe into league with Germany against us. On his return from Budapest he had pleaded in vain for a conference with the leaders of Central Europe, *as they were unanimously asking for*, with a view to *economic cooperation and reconstruction*,[50] but nothing had been done. He confirmed his absolute refusal to serve on the Austrian Commission. Looking back later, he noted *how near I was to a break with Lloyd George.*[51]

But Lloyd George was ever fertile in devices to avert a crisis and not above artifice. On 28 May Smuts received a mysterious message from Philip Kerr, Lloyd George's secretary. The Prime Minister, wrote Kerr, was much impressed by Smuts's views but was not in a position to explain at present. Smuts was sceptical, suspecting that Lloyd George was playing a double game, and he declined to be his dupe. At best, he wrote to Margaret Gillett, *the Prime Minister wants to ride to heaven on the back of the devil, and he hails me on the way: 'My dear General, you get hold of the tail of this fellow and he will carry us a good way. If we come across Christian* [the hero of John Bunyan's *Pilgrim's Progress* (1678)] *walking another way to heaven, we can let go and join Christian's company!'*[52]

6

'Wilson Peace' or 'Scrap of Paper'?
29 May–2 June 1919

At the end of May began the fourth and final chapter of Smuts's struggle at the Peace Conference. *I feel as if the next month or two months are big with fate,*[1] he wrote to Alice Clark, and to Isie: *Let us hope that all will yet come right before the end.*[2] In the three weeks since the presentation of the Treaty, the Germans had forwarded a succession of comments on its individual chapters. On 29 May, the deadline laid down by the Allies, they submitted a final memorandum of *Observations* on the Treaty as a whole, together with a set of counter-proposals. Contrasting the terms laid down by the Allies with 'the Wilson peace' held out in the President's Points, Principles, Ends and Particulars, they offered a number of important voluntary concessions based on those legally binding declarations: the transfer to France, subject to a plebiscite, of Alsace-Lorraine; military disarmament, and naval disarmament well beyond the limits demanded, provided that the Allies reciprocated; territorial cessions to Poland on strict lines of nationality, to include most of the province of Posen (Poznan), together with road and rail access

PRINCIPLES, ENDS AND PARTICULARS

President Wilson's most famous speech was that of 8 January 1918, the Fourteen Points speech, but he insisted, and the Germans and the Allies agreed, that the peace must also be based on three other of his 1918 speeches.

On 11 February he defined his Four Principles as:

- That every part of the settlement must be based on justice and contribute to a permanent peace.
- That 'peoples and provinces are not to be bartered about from sovereignty to sovereignty'.
- That 'every territorial settlement involved in this war must be made in the interest and for the benefit of the populations concerned'.
- That 'all well defined national aspirations shall be accorded the utmost satisfaction'.

On 4 July he delivered his Four Ends speech. These were:

- The destruction or weakening of every arbitrary power that threatens peace.
- The free acceptance by the people involved of the territorial, political and economic arrangements of the settlement.
- The need for modern civilized states to behave with the same codes of conduct and honour and respect for the law as is expected of their citizens.
- The establishment of a new international organization to deal with disputes between states.

He summed up the Four Ends as 'What we seek is the reign of law, based upon the consent of the governed and sustained by the organized opinion of mankind'.

The Five Particulars of 27 September were:

- The need for impartial justice for all the parties in the war.
- Fair treatment, without special privileges, for all.
- No special groupings or alliances within the family of the League of Nations.
- No special selfish economic arrangements within the League.
- The open publication of all treaties and international agreements.

Reflecting on Wilson's Fourteen Points, Clemenceau cynically observed: 'Fourteen points: that's a bit much. The Good Lord only had ten.'

to the Baltic (as Smuts had proposed) at Danzig, Königsberg and Memel; coal supplies to France from the Saar until the French mines were working again; assistance in the work of restoring the devastated war zone, and a counter-offer on reparations of £5 billion.

This was conditional on Germany's admission to the League of Nations, the restoration to her of her colonies as a Mandatory Power and the free expression of German self-determination through plebiscites in Austria and the Sudetenland. These counter-proposals were presented as the practical application of the conditions agreed at the Armistice. Back in February, the President of the new republican Germany, Friedrich Ebert, had thrown down a challenge to the Allies as they began their work: 'In reliance upon President Wilson's Fourteen Points Germany laid down her arms. Now give us the Wilson peace to which we have a claim.' [3]

'The Wilson peace' was a phrase which haunted Smuts. On 30 May, he received a copy of the German *Observations*, which he compared *very carefully*[4] with the draft Treaty. He was deeply impressed. The *Observations*, he wrote to Alice Clark, contained *a most powerful statement of the German case*: *They raise the point to the very forefront which I have always considered vital, viz., that we are bound by the correspondence of last October and November to make a Wilson peace – that is, one within the four corners of the Wilson Points and speeches. This was a solemn international engagement which we must keep. It would be dreadful if, while the war began with a 'scrap of paper', it were also to end with another 'scrap of paper' and the Allies' breach of their own undertaking. I am going to fight it out on this basis.*[5]

His mind was made up. He would not sign the terms as they stood. Margaret Gillett sent words of encouragement: 'I feel I know enough of what signing means to make me believe you cannot do it and ever have peace in your own being over your own life.' However much as a Quaker she had disapproved of his participation in the War, 'I believed it possible that in God's hands such a step might bring you where you would be immensely useful to Europe.' [6]

Smuts wrote a final letter to President Wilson. Subject only to the proviso in the Pre-Armistice Agreement on damage to civilians, the peace, he pointed out, must be *a Wilson peace*, based exclusively on the Fourteen Points. *To my mind there is absolutely no doubt that this is so*, he wrote. Anything beyond or outside the Points should be eliminated from the Treaty as a *breach of agreement*. It was said, he continued, that if Wilson himself was satisfied with the terms, who could gainsay him? This, Smuts diplomatically observed, was *to put the whole responsibility* on the President. It was *most unfair to you*. The question for the peacemakers was a simple one: *whether our Peace Treaty is within the four corners of your Speeches of 1918. Frankly I do not think this is so.* [7] Wilson replied briefly but non-committally, suggesting that he, Lloyd George and Clemenceau were 'quite willing to re-study some of the conclusions formerly reached' and that the coming week might produce 'some important decisions'. [8] There was no further contact at Paris between Smuts and Wilson.

The British Delegation debates the Treaty

The next and final stage, viewed in the long perspective, was one of the most crucial of the Conference and a defining moment in what has been called the 'pre-history of appeasement'. Smuts braced himself for a supreme challenge: to persuade his colleagues in the British Empire Delegation, which, he heard, would shortly be called together in Plenary Session, to his way of thinking. He abandoned plans for a weekend meeting with the Gilletts in London, fearing, as he informed Margaret, that *in my absence the Prime Minister might call a meeting of British Delegates. And I want to be there when we discuss our line of action.*[9] Though oppressed by a sense of *impending calamity,*[10] he wrote, *I say to myself that it is cowardly to admit and submit to defeat, that up to the last moment we must exhaust every means in our power to right the situation.*[11] Lloyd George too had recognised that a critical moment had come. He summoned to Paris as many of his Cabinet colleagues as could be spared to attend a day of joint meetings with the Empire Delegation on Sunday 1 June for the purpose of considering the German objections.

On Friday 30 May, the Empire Delegates convened for a preliminary discussion: the Dominion representatives, including Smuts, representing South Africa in Botha's temporary absence; the Prime Minister, the Foreign Secretary, the two other British Plenipotentiaries, Milner and Barnes, and Lord Robert Cecil. Smuts spoke first. He put his case with force and conviction. He rested it on one simple fact: the Allies were *bound to make a peace within the four corners of the Fourteen Points.*[12] When the two rednecks of the Delegation, Massey and Hughes, poured cold water on this and even Balfour expressed scepticism, Smuts insisted that the point was *very serious and should be considered very seriously.*[13]

The Prime Minister's Cabinet colleagues in the Coalition reached Paris the next day: Lord Chancellor Birkenhead, Secretary of State for War Churchill, the Chancellor of the Exchequer Austen Chamberlain, and two Liberal members of the Government, the Secretary of State for India Edwin Montagu and the President of the Board of Education Herbert Fisher. They joined Lloyd George for dinner in his flat. 'After dinner,'

Fisher wrote in his diary, 'we sit in a hemicircle [*sic*] and L-G asks us in turn what criticisms we have of the Treaty ... We all condemn the Treaty and agree that it should be modified.'[14] 'The whole drift of the conversation,' Montagu confirmed, 'was unanimous.'[15] Their conclusions were radical: the Allies should drop the Polish Corridor, reduce the length of the Saar and Rhineland occupations, grant Germany early admission to the League and make 'a drastic revision of the reparation clauses'. £5 billion was suggested 'as the total liability'.[16] Discussion continued until midnight and resumed next morning at one of Lloyd George's 'working breakfasts'. Concession was urged again, and Fisher confirmed, 'We all condemn the Treaty and agree that it should be modified.'[17] Lloyd George, according to Montagu, was 'very much impressed'.[18]

The meetings so far, formal and informal, thus went well for the revisionists. But it was the two Plenary Sessions on Sunday 1 June that were to prove decisive. *I am deeply interested*, Smuts wrote to Margaret Gillett before leaving for the Prime Minister's flat, *to know whether any, and how many, others will share my rather strong views.*[19] Discussion began at 11 a.m., broke for the afternoon and resumed in the evening.

Again Smuts spoke first and at length. He 'violently denounced the Treaty,' noted Montagu, describing it as *an impossible document*. To sign it, he said, would be *a real disaster, comparable in magnitude to that of the war itself.*[20] The German objections were *perfectly sound*. The Allies were bound to make *a Wilson peace*. He challenged *any lawyer to go through the correspondence with the Germans before the Armistice and then say that the Allies were not bound to make a peace on Wilson's terms and on the basis of his speeches. The Allies must keep their agreement* and not treat the Pre-Armistice Agreement as *another scrap of paper*. This was *not a mere matter of form or a technical legal question:* it was *one of vital substance.* That was his *first and fundamental point,* for the Treaty, he said, *bristled with provisions which were outside the Fourteen Points* and others *which were inconsistent with the Fourteen Points.*[21]

In January 1918, Smuts reminded them, the Prime Minister had proclaimed Britain's war aims to the world. Smuts regarded these declarations as *bedrock and as governing any treaty.* The draft Treaty *would make a bad peace. It was not just and it would not be durable.* Indeed it contained *the roots of war.*[22] The Rhineland occupation was *quite unnecessary* and *indefensible from every point of view.* The territorial arrangements in west and east alike were *thoroughly bad.* He was glad to hear general agreement that the eastern frontiers must be revised, for by subjecting Germans to Polish rule, he said, *we were putting the Germans under a lot of Kaffirs.*[23] Germany should join the League from the outset. On reparations, he favoured *fixing a definite sum, say £5 billion,* which *should be divided now between the Allies, each of whom should use its own part as it pleased.* That would obviate further sterile argument about the meaning of civilian damage. Lloyd George interrupted to point out that 'the French would not accept the British proposals for a division'. Smuts ended by stating that as the Treaty stood he could not *vote for it* and he doubted whether he *could sign it.*[24]

Most of those present agreed with Smuts on particular aspects of the Treaty and all agreed about the Polish frontiers. Even Hughes agreed that the Germans had 'a good case'[25] there. Churchill urged them to give the Prime Minister a free hand to reach what he called 'a "split the difference" peace'[26] and Birkenhead and Montagu agreed. Chamberlain viewed the Rhineland occupation 'with the same dread as General

Smuts'.[27] On reparations, the Prime Minister was still talking of £11 billion. Chamberlain 'did not believe that it was possible to get £11 billion out of Germany, or anything like it'. He was 'very strongly of the opinion of General Smuts'[28] that the Allies should name a fixed sum and divide it between them. Sir George Foster, the Canadian representative, concurred. He 'would make the sum as moderate as possible'.[29] He too believed that Germany should be admitted to the League.

'The strangest thing about the proceeding,' Montagu noted, 'was the unanimity.'[30] Everyone urged some concession or other. But only Barnes and Montagu, two relative 'lightweights', sided openly with Smuts in his central objection that the peace was not *a Wilson peace*. Barnes said he was 'in hearty agreement with General Smuts regarding the general character'[31] of the Treaty. No-one else accepted this or supported Smuts's contention that the Allies could not introduce terms that *were not covered by the Fourteen Points* or that *went beyond the Fourteen Points*.[32]

Lloyd George and Balfour, sitting together on a sofa, made common cause against Smuts. Balfour focused on the core of Smuts's argument. He conceded that 'if the Fourteen Points were pressed from a legal point of view, it was possible to make out an awkward case'. He claimed, however, that it was 'impossible to interpret the Fourteen Points and the supplementary speeches as if they constituted a contract between two litigants'.[33] Balfour's prestige, exquisite courtesy and air of sweet reason were persuasive; and no-one pointed out that he was talking nonsense, or suggested that a lawyer of Smuts's calibre might know better. Lord Chancellor Birkenhead, a brilliant legal mind, said little, and on this, the fundamental issue, nothing at all.

When the meeting resumed in the evening, Balfour returned

to the attack with the same insidious charm. While he suavely described Smuts's criticisms as 'most impressive and important', he 'could not help thinking,' he repeated, 'that General Smuts treated the matter in rather too legal a manner.' It was 'impossible' to interpret the Fourteen Points 'literally and to make a contract out of them'.[34] Foster agreed, though he thought 'President Wilson could justify the main part of the Treaty on the Fourteen Points and his speeches'.[35] But it was Hughes who hit the nail resoundingly on the head. 'The Germans had not a leg to stand on,' he said. For if, as Smuts contended, the terms were really inconsistent with Wilson's Principles, they 'might very well leave it to President Wilson to say so'. The President 'would be the last man' to approve anything less than a Wilson peace. Lloyd George had already pressed this home, confirming that 'the President maintained that the draft treaty was a fair exposition of the Fourteen Points'.[36] Here, undoubtedly, Smuts was at his most vulnerable. His case was undermined by these thrusts. What better authority on *a Wilson peace* than Wilson himself?

So Smuts failed to persuade the majority of his colleagues of the Treaty's incompatibility with the Fourteen Points or that it mattered. He had right on his side, and law, but that was not enough. Despite the clarity, vigour and patent sincerity of his presentation, and what Nicolson called his 'tremendous dignity',[37] he had not found the right words to sway these men. Talk of justice for Germany did not move men who knew only too well what Germany had done and at what terrible cost. They were there to ensure that never again would Germany unleash such destruction. They were willing to make pragmatic concessions to secure a signature; but they felt in their bones that Germany deserved a harsh peace, and Smuts's insistence on the legal aspect of the question left them cold.

Smuts's logic was impeccable; his psychology was flawed. He struck the wrong note by insisting on what seemed dry legalities (though how else he could have made the point is hard to say); and one example which he repeatedly chose to stress was weak and unconvincing: the internationalisation of Germany's rivers. Several took him up on it. While Smuts's point was pertinent, his identification of it as a provision that *should be scrapped altogether*[38] was not an issue to stir the blood. Lloyd George, with his hawk's eye for an opponent's weakness, swooped on it and picked it clean. He did not think, he said, that Smuts 'had done justice' to the issue. Poland and Czechoslovakia and for that matter Alsace-Lorraine, needed guaranteed access to the sea and 'it was therefore quite right to have international control' of what were 'international rivers'.[39]

Smuts's appeals for justice as legality thus lacked emotional compulsion. Lloyd George, that consummate political tactician, had pounced on this from the start. Following Balfour's lead, he elaborated the point and turned it against Smuts. He agreed, he said, that 'it was possible to establish a technical injustice on the basis of the Fourteen Points, but that was not going to make any difference in the eyes of the world if it was not a real injustice'.[40] This was a forensic masterstroke, crushing in its insight and effectiveness. For all his careful advocacy, Smuts failed to carry his fundamental point, while the Prime Minister and the Foreign Secretary contrived to make it seem irrelevant and quixotic. They wrong-footed Smuts and destroyed his credibility.

Besides, as Smuts realised, the British Delegation was weary of the Conference, drawn out long beyond all expectations. They wanted an end to it and the Dominion Delegates wanted to go home. He noted a strong tendency to say,

'*Oh, do let us have peace and begin afresh; the Treaty does not really matter so much; and in any case let the League of Nations amend it hereafter if it is unworkable.*'[41] Against this prevailing mood Smuts could make no headway. Thus while 'on the whole,' as Milner noted, 'the opinions expressed were strongly critical of the Peace terms',[42] Smuts found no effectual support. *You see how isolated I am at present*,[43] he had written to Margaret Gillett a fortnight before.

Moreover his political position was inherently weak. Since his resignation from the War Cabinet six months before, he was only *the second representative of South Africa*,[44] and even then he could not speak unequivocally for South Africa. Botha himself was present at the Sunday meetings. He said little, save to remind 'my dear friend Milner' that it was 17 years almost to the day that the Peace of Vereeniging was signed. Botha's *memories of that awful moment*, Smuts recalled, *blended with pity for the Germans*.[45] 'It was moderation,' said Botha, 'which had saved South Africa for the British Empire' and he 'hoped that on this occasion it would be moderation which would save the world'.[46] Botha *did not wear his heart on his sleeve*, wrote Smuts, *but in the background was this fundamental faith, and on certain testing occasions it revealed itself visibly in his behavior.*[47] This was such an occasion.

Botha's brief intervention, Fisher agreed, was a 'remarkable

THE SIGNING OF THE TREATY
At the signing of the Treaty of Versailles on 28 June 1919, Botha surveyed the whole scene, said Smuts, and bending over his agenda paper, wrote on it the following words: 'God's judgments will be done with justice to all peoples under the new sun, and we shall persevere in the prayer that they may be done to mankind in charity and peace and a Christian spirit.' These words now hang in the Prime Minister's room at the Union Buildings in Pretoria. Two months later, on 27 August, Botha died suddenly, aged 57, and Smuts became Prime Minister of South Africa.

moment',[48] but it was oblique, a moral exhortation, not a critique of the Treaty. In that respect Smuts received no help from his chief. Whether Botha's support would have made any difference cannot be known; but its absence visibly weakened Smuts's authority. *I am not in charge*, Smuts wrote, *and certainly go farther than the rest, though many have grave misgivings and would go a great distance.*[49] Even with Botha's support, it is unlikely that Smuts could have prevailed against what Montagu called the 'honourable woodenheadedness'[50] of the New Zealand representative, Prime Minister Massey, or the irksome obduracy of Hughes, 'the ineffable Hughes', as Cecil called him.[51] In any event Smuts did not prevail against the Prime Minister and Foreign Secretary in concert. Together they had turned his flank. Now Balfour rolled it up. He 'begged the Delegation to leave absolute discretion to the Prime Minister'.[52]

Lloyd George was prepared to accept some modifications of the terms, some changes to provisions on which he had himself entertained doubts since the time of the Fontainebleau Memorandum. On the Polish frontiers he was for plebiscites, he favoured Germany's early admission to the League and some reduction in the Rhineland occupation. At the close of the final meeting, he adroitly presented these proposals, in the form of a resolution, as a summary of the discussion and the feeling of the meeting, and asked for formal authority to put them to Wilson and Clemenceau. Birkenhead said that it was 'the unanimous opinion of the Delegation that the Prime Minister should be armed with the large powers which he suggested'.[53]

7

'The Last Battle of the War': June 1919

The night following these final deliberations was a fitful one for Smuts. *I could not sleep*, he wrote to Margaret Gillett, *with this great trouble on my mind*. Lloyd George's concessions – *which I consider paltry* – were nowhere near enough to satisfy him and fell far short of his insistence on a *Wilson peace*. This *document*, he repeated, *I cannot sign in its present form*.[1]

He also believed the consensus at the discussions had been skewed by Lloyd George. At the time Smuts had not objected to the Prime Minister's summing-up. Having taken the lead in attacking the Treaty, he may have felt that further intervention on his part would be counter-productive. However, when a formal minute, based on that summing-up, was circulated after the meeting, Smuts sent Lloyd George another powerful protest.

The proposed modifications to the Treaty as set out in the minute, he wrote, did less than justice to the opposition voiced by half a dozen speakers who favoured *substantial amendment*. The minute, he stated, *cannot be allowed to pass unchallenged*. Whatever happened, he himself would

It is useless to deny that I am filled with disappointment and grief at the way things are going. My own unremitting efforts behind the scenes for the last two and a half years seem doomed to failure. At the vital moment there seems to be a failure of leadership, and also a failure of the general human spirit among the peoples. I hope I am wrong, but I have a sense of impending calamity, a fear that the war was only the vanguard of calamity ... I cannot look at that draft treaty without a sense of grief and shame.

J C SMUTS TO LADY MARY MURRAY, WIFE OF GILBERT MURRAY, CLASSICIST AND SUPPORTER OF THE LEAGUE OF NATIONS, 2 JUNE 1919[2]

continue to dissent: *So far as I myself am concerned, I wish to make it clear that I cannot agree to anything less than the very drastic course I proposed.* He insisted that *the Peace Treaty should be recast and transformed, so as to be more in accord with our solemn undertakings, our public declarations, and the requirements of a reasonable and practicable policy.* He again stipulated Germany's immediate admission to the League, no Rhineland occupation, a *thorough revision* of the borders with Poland, *the fixing of a reasonable though high amount* in reparations and a review of the powers of the Reparations Commission, *which constitute a serious invasion of German sovereignty ... This programme,* he concluded, *I must stand by.*[3]

Smuts and Lloyd George were now at daggers drawn. Relations between them were 'so strained', according to one of the Prime Minister's Cabinet Secretaries, 'that they refused to meet each other at lunch'.[4] The next day, 3 June, Lloyd George took Smuts to task in an angry, hard-hitting reply. He denied Smuts's account of the sense of the meeting and he rammed

home his own version. His summary and the resolution had
been unanimously approved. No-one spoke against it: 'You
made no remarks upon it yourself, though you had ample
opportunity.'[5] He challenged Smuts yet again to 'specify the
provisions which are not in accord with the Wilson formulas,
and how they should be amended'. What did Smuts mean by
a *reasonable, though high, amount of reparation* and how
was it to be exacted if not by the Reparation Commission,
backed by the sanction of military occupation? How should
it be allocated among the Allies? 'Are you prepared to forego
the claims for pensions?' he added nastily, and in a Parthian
shot he asked whether Smuts favoured returning South-West
Africa or Tanganyika to the Germans 'as a concession which
might induce them to sign the peace?'[6]

The last battle of the war is being fought out in Paris,
Smuts wrote to Margaret Gillett, *and we look like losing that
battle and with it the whole war.*[7] He replied to Lloyd George
the next day. However loosely the Fourteen Points were inter-
preted, he put it to the Prime Minister that the principle of
national self-determination was manifestly violated in the
clauses on the Saarland, Danzig and Memel, *indisputably
German territories with German populations, which we have
no right under those formulas to tear off Germany, either
permanently or temporarily.*[8] Attempts by local separatists
with French support to set up an independent Rhineland state
already showed the lack of wisdom of an occupation which
Smuts had always held to be *the most dangerous provision of
the whole Treaty.*[9] There was no more need to make Danzig
a Free City for the sake of Poland's access to the sea than to
create a free Hamburg for Czechoslovakia's. He proposed far
greater use of plebiscites in territory disputed between Poland
and Germany. On reparations they should *cut the Gordian*

knot and fix a total of around £5 billion, £2 billion to go to restoration in France and Belgium, the rest to be divided among the Allies to cover *other claims, such as pensions.*[10]

He repudiated with great dignity the Prime Minister's sneer over German South-West Africa: *Please do not have the impression that I would be generous at the expense of others so long as the Union gets South West Africa! In this great business South West Africa is as dust in the balance compared to the burdens now hanging over the civilized world.* He concluded with an earnest appeal for *the spirit of fair play and moderation: Perhaps the main difference between us is that you are struggling in the water, while I shout advice from the shore! But I feel deeply that this is no time to mince matters. When you are up against a position so terrible in its possibilities for good and evil, you can only do one thing, even if you fail utterly. And that is the right thing, the thing you can justify to your own conscience and that of all other reasonable, fair-minded people. This Treaty breathes a poisonous spirit of revenge, which may yet scorch the fair face – not of a corner of France, but of Europe.*[11]

But Smuts still stood alone. *I am not looked upon with special favour after the line I have taken*, he told Alice Clark, adding bitterly, *small men prefer sycophants.*[12] No-one was prepared to join him in openly opposing the Prime Minister. Botha shared Smuts's misgivings but *does not go as far as I want to go.*[13]

I am not yet sure what I am going to do, Smuts had written to Isie a fortnight earlier. *So my mind swings from one side to another.*[14] Besides, his home and his heart were elsewhere. He yearned for *the sunshine and the wide spaces of South Africa.*[15] He compared himself to Odysseus, homesick for Ithaca. He had been away for three-and-a-half years. All this time he had barely seen Isie and the children. In 1917 he had thought of himself as a man *on active service for humanity*.[16] He still saw himself in that role. He had broached with Isie the possibility of mounting a campaign against the Treaty. But from what base? He had burned his boats in London when he resigned from the War Cabinet. *I have been long from home, far away from the base which I have to rely on*, he wrote to Margaret Gillett. *I have not been big or effective enough in the last two years to work to a new base and to appeal from a world platform*.[17] A year ago, Lloyd George had thought of making him Foreign Secretary. Had he not renounced a political career in England, he might now have been able *to occupy a position at the centre instead of on the periphery*.[18] Alice Clark agreed. 'If you had taken charge of the Foreign Office two years ago,' she wrote, 'the course of events might have been very different.'[19]

True, he might start again. *You can believe me*, he said later in South Africa, *there was some temptation not to come back*.[20] The King had confidentially asked him to stay on, in the eventual expectation of becoming Prime Minister.[21] He might align himself with Labour or the Asquithian Liberals, and he might become leader of either. Six weeks earlier two Labour spokesmen, Barnes and Henderson, had been *pressing me to stay in English politics. Henderson says the Labour Party will follow the Prime Minister if I am with him!*[22] On the other hand he was far from sure that a public campaign or *an out-and-out attack on the Treaty*[23] would be welcomed. Rather it seemed that if Germany refused to sign, public opinion would back a resumption of hostilities. The tragedy was cosmic: it transcended mere politics and suggested to Smuts some essential *failure of the general human spirit*.[24]

Meanwhile, what was he to do? His last letters to Lloyd

George had been a form of ultimatum and a warning of resistance: he would not sign unless ... Keynes wrote offering support. Yet could Smuts really persist, a lone dissenter, against the Empire Delegation, the Big Three, indeed the entire Conference? 'Be not righteous overmuch' – he knew the biblical injunction. He poured out his predicament to Isie, to Alice Clark and Margaret Gillett, to Keynes and to Botha. On 3 June, he wrote to Margaret Gillett that he was *not budging an inch*,[25] though he did not know what he would do. Friends and family urged him to stand firm. A week later he wrote to Keynes, *I have not yet made up my mind*.[26] Keynes himself had just resigned from the British Delegation in protest. Smuts added that whatever happened, *the Treaty will in any case emerge as a rotten thing, of which we shall all be heartily ashamed in due course*. Meanwhile the world desperately needed peace. It might be that with peace, *a great revulsion will set in and a favourable atmosphere will be created in which to help the public virtually to scrap this monstrous instrument*.[27]

The same day, he wrote again to Isie. He wavered between the call to action and a fatalistic acceptance. On the one hand he felt that he must fight *this death sentence on Europe*. On the other hand, *what is the use of all this toil? It will and must all soon collapse anyway. Leave this Treaty to its own devices, and it will soon come to an end. So my mind swings from one side to the other*.[28] He became less alarmed about the immediate prospects for Europe and his thoughts veered back towards acquiescence. *The only bright spot in a situation of unrelieved gloom*, he wrote to Margaret Gillett, was the League of Nations: *But my work there is done, and the mustard seed will grow through the coming ages*. As for the Treaty, he wrote of his *quiet but fundamental faith in God, the regenerative spirit* and his belief in the remedial effect of *time and tide.*[29]

But as the Allies made ready to invade Germany, Smuts again rebelled. *My mind is fully made up not to sign,* he cabled Botha, then in London, on 21 June, asking whether he should *resign as South African delegate so as not to embarrass you.*[30] To Margaret Gillett he repeated two days later, *I am not going to sign it on any account.* He did not know what would result, *and to some extent I don't care.*[31] Suddenly, overnight, he changed his mind. He had come to the simple realisation that he could not let down Botha. As head of delegation and Prime Minister, Botha had no choice. He must sign, to validate the legal recognition of South Africa's independent statehood, the object for which he and Smuts had fought throughout their political life since the Boer War, and to seal South Africa's title as the Mandatory for South-West Africa. So, as Smuts recalled, *Botha could not help me.*[32]

Moreover he knew Botha to be a sick man. Smuts had tried at the Conference to take on as much of his chief's work as he could in addition to his own. He would assist Botha on slow, painful walks. Botha 'would be leaning on Smuts's arm, while Smuts would be helping his old friend along tenderly'.[33] Smuts had no wish to appear holier than Botha – *people will think I am trying to put myself on a pedestal.*[34] If he resigned, it would be said in South Africa that the two were at odds and that either he or Botha was wrong. If he did not sign, he would split his party and play into the hands of Hertzog and the Nationalists. He would undo the work of unification which he and Botha had achieved in 17 years of partnership. Then came the news that after all the Germans had agreed to sign. Come what might, the Treaty was going to be signed. Nothing he might do would prevent that. What then could he achieve by standing out alone? Looked at in that light, there no longer seemed any choice. As at Vereeniging, he faced the inevitable. *After all I am going to sign that Treaty*, he wrote to Margaret Gillett on 24 June. *Any other course would make the position of General Botha (who must sign) indefensible and impossible.*[35]

Four days later came the scene so deeply etched in the historical memory of Europe: the signing of the Treaty in the Hall of Mirrors at Versailles. To Smuts the occasion was *uninspired, unimpressive, mechanical, soulless.*[36] He and Botha sat side by side at the table provided for the signing. Botha, surveying the scene, was moved to write on his agenda paper a prayer that God's judgment on all nations would be meted out 'in charity and peace and a Christian spirit'.[37] *At that moment*, Smuts recalled of his troubled, ailing chief, *when jubilation filled all hearts, he heard the undertone of the ages and felt only the deepest pity for the fate of human kind.*[38] *May God have mercy*, Smuts himself reflected, *on the victors as well as on the vanquished.*[39]

Smuts felt his own signature to be *a sacrificial act*. He felt for the two lone German signatories. *Not a word of sympathy for them at the end when one little word from Clemenceau or* [Lloyd] *George or Wilson would have meant so much*. Smuts had scrupulously asked Lloyd George *for permission to say a few words to express my feelings*. But Lloyd George, warning of *a very unpleasant scene*,[40] had advised against.

Smuts had long meditated an appeal to the public and a *campaign of reconciliation ... after the Peace Treaty has been signed*.[41] He was to issue two statements. He released the first immediately after he had signed. It appeared in the press the next day. *I have signed the Peace Treaty*, it began, *not because I consider it a satisfactory document, but because it is imperatively necessary to close the war; because the world needs peace above all.* He wrote, he said, in a phrase suggested by Margaret Gillett, *not in criticism but in faith … I feel that the real work of making peace will only begin after this Treaty has been signed.*

The promise of the new life, he continued, meaning the ideals of *a new international order and a fairer, better world, are not written in this Treaty.* 'Not in this mountain, nor in Jerusalem', he went on, quoting St John's Gospel, *'but in the spirit and in truth', as the Great Master said, must the foundations of the new order be laid.* Smuts called for *a new spirit of generosity and humanity, born in the hearts of the peoples,* as *the solvent for the problems which the statesmen have found too hard at the Conference.*[42]

Winston Churchill and J C Smuts, April 1945. Smuts was one of the few whose advice Churchill respected. 'My faith in Smuts is unbreakable,' he said.

III

The Legacy

8

'A Carthaginian Peace'? 1919–1939

I return to South Africa a defeated man,[1] said Smuts. Throughout the War he had followed with optimism and confidence a grail, *the vision of the New Earth* that would justify the sacrifice. *In Paris*, he confessed, *that vision vanished.*[2] He felt crushed by the forces beyond him. *I frankly admit I have lost some of my earlier optimism,*[3] he wrote to Alice Clark. Hitherto, he reflected, *I had always been successful ... Even the Boer war was a fatality through which, as a man, I came out strengthened. There was something grand in the struggle that elevated me. In Paris I saw my smallness against fate.*[4] The peacemakers had squandered the unrepeatable opportunity. *I had, like Job, cursed the whole lot of them,*[5] wrote Smuts; yet he accepted that he too was one of them, that he too had failed.

Smuts never ceased to regard the Treaty as an *abomination.*[6] Was he right? Was the Treaty really at variance with the *Wilson peace*, and if it was, did it really matter? Balfour, disdainful of anything resembling what he called 'a lawyer's argument',[7] objected that Smuts took too legalistic a view, and denied that the Allies were bound by the Pre-Armistice

Agreement. In so doing he flatly contradicted the view which Lloyd George, Clemenceau, Wilson and Balfour himself had unequivocally taken at the time, only half a year before, when they unanimously confirmed that, once accepted by Germany, the Pre-Armistice Agreement would bind both sides and that the Fourteen Points, subject to Lloyd George's proviso on reparations, constituted the legal basis of the peace. Balfour had insisted on this: 'We should certainly be bound,'[8] he had said then. The contractual nature of the Pre-Armistice Agreement was also expressly confirmed by the Allies in their formal reply to the German counter-proposals. On that, they declared, they were 'in complete accord with the German Delegation ... These are the principles upon which hostilities were abandoned in November 1918, these are the principles upon which the Allied and Associated Powers agreed that peace might be based.'[9] What could be clearer? The Fourteen Points, as Smuts said, were *bedrock*.[10]

Were the Fourteen Points, then, fairly and reasonably applied in the Treaty? The reader who has followed Smuts in his repeated remonstrances must surely agree that they were not, and that the imposition of such questionable terms on the most powerful state in a weakened and fissiparous Europe was unlikely to bring lasting peace. For it was the paradox of Versailles that it left Germany not merely aggrieved and vengeful but with both the motive and the means to rid herself of what she called the 'Treaty of Shame' and to recover a status commensurate with her demographic, economic and geopolitical potential. Versailles was not so much a peace as a standing provocation, and from its inception it contained, as Smuts pointed out, *the roots of war*.[11]

It was thus a singular misnomer when Smuts, in an

unfortunate allusion which still continues to reverberate, described Versailles as *this reactionary peace – the most reactionary since Scipio Africanus dealt with Carthage.*[12] The 'Carthaginian Peace' of 146 BC dealt Carthage its death-blow; while Germany after Versailles, still in Smuts's words, *the dominant factor* in Europe, was able to recover within a dozen years, to throw off the shackles of the Treaty, to resume under Adolf Hitler the challenge for mastery in Europe and in 1940 to reverse, with crushing ease and superiority, the verdict of 1919. Smuts believed the First World War had at least achieved *the destruction of Prussian militarism*;[13] but Versailles had scotched the snake, not killed it. The toxic mixture of German power, militarism and aggressive nationalism would re-emerge, vigorous, virulent, vicious and victorious, as Nazism. Far from being a 'Carthaginian Peace', Versailles, as Smuts put it, with greater accuracy, was a house of sand that *will and must all soon collapse anyway.*[14]

'A CARTHAGINIAN PEACE'
Smuts described the Treaty of Versailles as *this reactionary peace – the most reactionary since Scipio Africanus dealt with Carthage.* Ironically, the peace dictated by Scipio in 202 BC after the Second Punic War was in fact remarkably lenient. It was in 146 BC after the Third Punic War that the Romans imposed the true 'Carthaginian Peace': they destroyed the city of Carthage, slaughtered or enslaved its inhabitants and reputedly sowed the ground with salt so that nothing should grow there. The expression 'a Carthaginian Peace', applied by Smuts to the Treaty of Versailles, was made notorious by Keynes in *The Economic Consequences of the Peace* (1919).

Was Smuts, as the French complained, mistaken as to the German mentality? It had been assumed, said Balfour, 'that Germany was repentant, that her soul had undergone a conversion and that she was now absolutely a different nation'.[15] He for one saw no evidence of that. Would the magnanimous peace that Smuts urged have been a sufficient guarantee of Germany's good behaviour? It was one thing for Great Britain, at the height of her imperial power, to extend the hand of friendship to the *plucky little republics*,[16] the Transvaal and the Orange Free State, in 1906. It was another to trust that similar chivalry would be appreciated and reciprocated by a still powerful Germany that had come close to victory against a world in arms. Under the Weimar Republic, the upper classes, the army, civil service, judiciary and professoriat, unrepentant save at losing the War, still hankered after the Kaiser's Germany. Whether what Smuts called the *contagion of magnanimity*[17] would have proved beneficial in Germany's case, whether a true *Wilson peace* would have succeeded, is a matter for speculation. What cannot be doubted, as Smuts so clearly foresaw, was that the *Diktat* of Versailles was bound to weaken the authority of the democratic Republic of Weimar that signed it and the credibility of the liberal values for which it stood.

Smuts strove to impress on Lloyd George the inescapable corollary of German power: the fact that, like it or not, peace in Europe depended ultimately on German cooperation. Hence his pleas for a peace that would commend itself to moderate German opinion, would command genuine assent and would be executed in good faith. In a second public statement issued on the eve of his return to South Africa, he underlined these home truths. *The brutal fact*, he said, *is that Great Britain is a very small island on the fringe of the Continent, and that on the Continent the seventy-odd million Germans represent the most important and formidable national factor.* Hence, as he stressed, *the supreme importance to this country and to Europe of having a stable, moderate, democratic republic in Germany.* When, therefore, he concluded that *the word <u>reconciliation</u> has to be writ large on our skies*,[18] he not only enjoined *the great Christian qualities of mercy, pity and forgiveness*;[19] he also preached the most down-to-earth *Realpolitik.*

The great Christian qualities were less evident in Smuts's attitude to France. The French accused him of being pro-Boche – Clemenceau called him 'the saboteur of the Treaty of Versailles'[20] – and they were right. Smuts believed that the Treaty contained *far too much of the French demands,*[21] that Clemenceau had outwitted Wilson and Lloyd George and that France pursued an *arrogant diplomacy.*[22] In the memorandum which he drew up for Lloyd George in November 1918, 'Our Policy at the Peace Conference', Smuts portrayed post-war France as Britain's traditional rival, *a difficult if not an intolerable neighbour, ... ambitious ... militant and imperialist.* French policy, he foresaw, would be to *keep Germany in a state of humiliating subjection*, ill-attuned to *future peace and cooperation.*[24] Both Smuts and Botha, marked by their Boer War experiences, were more alive to the plight of the defeated enemy than to the security concerns of France, bled white by four years of German aggression, still vulnerable and still in fear of her redoubtable neighbour. Were the French mistaken in their craving for security? *Their best criticism*, Smuts said later, *was that I didn't understand the Germans and they did – they had the Germans for neighbours.*[25]

> **My own case is a striking instance of how the enemy of today may be the friend and comrade of tomorrow.**
>
> J C SMUTS'S FAREWELL STATEMENT ON RETURNING TO SOUTH AFRICA, 18 JULY 1919[23]

Both the Treaty and the League of Nations had been premised on American participation. America's repudiation of the League crippled it from the outset so that the League, as Smuts put it, *was left on Europe's doorstep.*[26] Wilson was to blame for his disastrous failure to secure ratification by the United States Senate in November 1919 and again in March 1920. *I remember saying to him,* said Smuts, <u>*Can*</u> *you carry the treaty?* <u>*Can*</u> *you get your two-thirds majority?* 'I absolutely can,' replied Wilson.[27] *He has failed democracy,* Smuts wrote to Alice Clark in the immediate bitterness of Paris – *the man who was to make the world safe for democracy.*[28] To C P Scott he described Wilson as *a second-rate man,* who *handled the whole business without adequate knowledge or resolution.* Yet *in spite of his weakness and folly,* he held Wilson to be a noble and tragic figure, and his League of Nations, he believed, *would remain and in time would win its way.*[29] In a later judgement of the President's role at Paris, he wrote: *It was not Wilson who failed there, but humanity itself.*[30]

As for Lloyd George, he was *all right in 1917 and all right in 1918* as a war-leader, Smuts agreed, *down to the moment of the General Election,* after which he was *unstable without any clear guiding principle, jumping about from one position to another.*[32] Balfour was *a tragedy, a mere dilettante, without force or guidance, when a strong British Foreign Minister might have saved the whole*

'Smuts comes and talks to me after dinner. He deplores the influence of French "shell-shock" upon the peace. I say that after all this *has been* a shell, there *is* a shell, and there *will remain* a shell. He says it is jingoism none the less and that it has ruined the fine spirit in which we came to Paris. There is something in what he says. Paris was not a good place for the Conference ... I quite admit that the French cannot see beyond their noses; but after all they are *their* noses: and, my word, what they *do* see, they see damned clearly.'

HAROLD NICOLSON, DIARY, 1 MAY 1919[31]

situation.[33] Smuts himself, as he knew, might have been that Foreign Minister.

On quitting the Conference, Keynes wrote to Smuts, hoping he would agree that 'some public explanation of what is really happening and a protest against it is the right course. If so, I am at your service.'[34] Smuts replied, encouraging Keynes to write *a clear connected account of what the financial and economic clauses of the Treaty actually are and mean, and what their probable results will be*.[35] A month later, he had second thoughts. Cautioning Keynes against *a regular attack on the Treaty*, he advised, *Better to be constructive*.[36] It was too late. Keynes had the bit between his teeth. *The Economic Consequences of the Peace*, that shattering polemic against the Treaty, appeared in December 1919 with worldwide repercussions. It included the damning description of Versailles, borrowed from Smuts, as 'a Carthaginian Peace'.

Smuts was dismayed by the personal note in Keynes's book. *Its brilliant belittlement of the great leaders, and chiefly Woodrow Wilson*,[37] was harmful and counterproductive. The caricature of Wilson as gullible and out of his depth *made an Aunt Sally of the noblest figure – perhaps the only noble figure – in the history of the war. It helped to finish Wilson, and it strengthened the Americans against the League*.[38]

Prime Minister of South Africa 1919–1924

Though tempted by the prospect of Treaty revision and a commanding role at the League of Nations from a political base in Britain, Smuts returned to South Africa. *In the end*, he said, *I came back because of Botha*.[39] A month later, Botha was dead. Smuts succeeded him as leader of the South African Party, Prime Minister, Minister of Defence and Minister of Native Affairs. He rose to the challenge with all his accustomed vigour and resolve, facing a combination of economic recession, violent industrial unrest and anti-Indian feeling. He justified discrimination against Indians on pragmatic grounds: *You cannot give rights to the Indians which you deny to the rest of the coloured citizens in South Africa*,[40] he said. This exposed him to obvious charges of hypocrisy from liberals, while as ever, he faced rancorous opposition from Hertzog's Nationalists and bore much personal abuse in dignified silence.

Smuts continued to hanker after a Greater South Africa that would also include Southern Rhodesia. In 1922 the British government gave Rhodesia that option in a plebiscite, but to Smuts's disappointment Rhodesia voted to become an autonomous Crown Colony. Likewise he continued to hope South Africa would take over Bechuanaland (Botswana), Basutoland (Lesotho) and Swaziland. Incorporation was provided for in the 1909 Act of Union, but the British Government confirmed that no transfer would take place against the wishes of the inhabitants (all are now independent states).

In the general election of 1920 the National Party overtook the South African Party on a cry of secession from the Empire, and Smuts became dependent on the pro-imperial Unionist Party, widely seen as representing the mine-owners. The two parties merged and won the next election with a large majority. A fall in the value of gold led to the increasing employment of low-wage black mineworkers, which in 1922 provoked violent disorder in Johannesburg at the hands of 20,000 white mineworkers. As in 1914, the disturbances took on revolutionary overtones. As then, Smuts reacted boldly. He again declared martial law and taking personal command of 7,000 troops supported by tanks and aeroplanes, he crushed the strike in three days at the cost of much bloodshed and several death sentences which he refused to commute, earning, as he wrote bitterly, *an additional claim to the titles of butcher and hangman*.[41] Alice Clark broke with him forever over the bloodletting. He was already under attack for the forcible suppression of two unauthorised native gatherings. In 1924, he called a general election and lost it to an unlikely combination of Labour and the Afrikaner Nationalists. Hertzog became Prime Minister and for the first time in 17 years Smuts found himself out of office.

Ireland, and France's Occupation of the Ruhr

So often a prophet without honour in his own country, Smuts was still held in great esteem and affection in Britain. Here, a reaction against Versailles was having its impact on foreign policy in a certain distancing from France, a sense of Germany as a force for stability in a chaotic Central and Eastern Europe and a rampart against Bolshevism. Smuts had followed up from South Africa the advice he had proffered to Europe in his public statements after the signing of the Treaty: he appealed to the Commonwealth for economic relief in Europe and he appointed Lord Robert Cecil and Gilbert Murray to represent South Africa at the League of Nations and to press for Germany's membership.

Smuts was in London for the Imperial Conference of 1921. His prestige was as high as ever, and he was back in favour with Lloyd George. Southern Ireland was in rebellion and in its efforts to crush the rebels, rogue elements in the British Army resorted to reprisals. Mindful of Britain's 'methods of barbarism' in the Boer War, Smuts warned Lloyd George that his policy was *an unmeasured calamity* and *a negation of all the principles of government*[42] to which the Commonwealth subscribed. He appealed for conciliation and he recommended Dominion status for the south. His visit came at a propitious moment. King George V was due to open the Parliament of the newly autonomous Northern Ireland at Belfast. Smuts advised that the King should *use the occasion to address himself to the whole of Ireland.*[43] His advice was taken. The King's speech to Stormont, based on a draft by Smuts, was well received and it helped smooth the way towards a truce with the south. Smuts, whose Boer War credentials made him acceptable to Sinn Féin, went secretly to Dublin to meet Eamon De Valera, and a ceasefire followed three days later. *I have brought both mules to the water*, he wrote before returning to South Africa, *but the drinking is their own affair.*[44] Anglo-Irish negotiations led in December to the conclusion of the Anglo-Irish Treaty and the granting of Dominion status to the Irish Free State, as Smuts had advocated.

Smuts continued to regret the artificial imbalance imposed at Versailles. *The great, the real mistake which was made at the Peace Conference*, he wrote to Lloyd George in 1922, *was to recognise the division of Europe into two camps and to exclude our enemies from the League.*[45] He remained critical of France. He resisted proposals to renew the Anglo-French Alliance and to give France the coveted military commitment. In November 1922 he wrote to Lloyd George's successor, Bonar Law: *French policy was for centuries the curse of Europe ... Now that Germany is down and out, the French are out for world power.* This was an exaggeration: it remained fear of German resurgence that motivated France; but it was true that, cheated of the promised treaties of guarantee from Britain and America, France looked for a chance to occupy the Ruhr, and Germany's default in paying reparations was *a cloak for the dismemberment of Germany.*[46] Such a policy was far beyond France's capacity, however, and Smuts was right to condemn it as untenable.

When French troops duly occupied the Ruhr in 1923, Smuts, in London for another Imperial Conference in October, resolved, as he wrote to Isie, to *bell the cat* and *damn the consequences.*[47] He denounced the French occupation as illegal; he made a strong plea to Britain to grasp the nettle of reparations; and he appealed to America for help in reaching an international agreement that should combine settlement of reparations with withdrawal from the Ruhr. Again, as at the Peace Conference, he drew the moral of his Boer past: *Defeated, broken, utterly exhausted, my little people also had to bow to the will of the conqueror.* But *the Boers were not treated as moral pariahs and outcasts. Decent human relationships were re-established and a spirit of mutual understanding grew up ... In the end simple human fellow feelings solved the problems which had proved too difficult for statesmanship.*[48]

Ostensibly Smuts spoke only as Prime Minister of South Africa. But he commanded enhanced attention as the one survivor of the leading men of the Peace Conference still in office. His intervention, warmly welcomed except in France, heralded the international conference that led to the Dawes Plan, which linked a more satisfactory settlement of reparations with a French withdrawal from the Ruhr; and the Locarno Treaties, which guaranteed the 1919 frontiers in the West, and led to the brief Locarno era of international amity between 1925 and 1929. In 1926 Germany at last joined the League of Nations. In 1929, at a dinner in London for the veterans of the East Africa campaign, Smuts toasted the guest of honour, none other than his old rival, von Lettow-Vorbeck, hailing the encounter as a symbol of post-war reconciliation.

Again, his insistence that *human nature is the same in all continents* blurred the difference between his *little people*[49] in South Africa and the 70 million-strong German state, already flexing its muscles again. But Smuts's basic point was sound: no lasting peace in Europe was possible without German goodwill.

Holism and Coalition

His years in opposition enabled Smuts to spend longer at Doornkloof and to give time to his scholarly pursuits. Smuts was very much more than a gifted amateur. A man of science – Albert Einstein said he was one of the few who really understood the theory of relativity – and a distinguished botanist in his own right, he became President of the South African Association for the Advancement of Science.

In 1926 he published the outcome of ideas which he had pondered since his student days. In *Holism and Evolution*, he offered his insights into science, history and life as movements tending towards healing and wholeness in the individual, the nation and the world. He believed that some guiding principle lay *at the heart of things and in the nature of this universe which is not a mere chance or random assemblement of items.*[50] An ordeal of suffering, such as he had endured in the Boer War and its aftermath, could serve to purge and recast the individual personality into something strong and harmonious, at peace with itself and others. He still hoped the experience of the First World War could bring about genuine reconciliation between the nations. *The principles of holism*, in his words, were *that in this universe we are all members of one another and that selfishness is the grand refusal and denial of life.*[51] In 1930 he became a Fellow of the Royal Society and in 1931 President of the British

Association for the Advancement of Science in its centenary year, an honour which he considered among the greatest of his life. Six years later he became Chancellor of the University of Cape Town.

In 1933, in the face of the world economic crisis and South Africa's abandonment, at Smuts's instigation, of the gold standard, Smuts and Hertzog joined in a government of national unity, merging their parties to form the South African National United Party (later the United Party). Smuts served under Hertzog as Deputy Prime Minister. This was a sacrifice on his part, for he would probably have won a general election had he called one; and Hertzog and the Nationalists strained his patience with their continual anti-Commonwealth clamour. *My Cabinet colleagues*, he admitted, *sometimes get on my nerves.*[52] On several issues where his liberal instincts were challenged, Smuts remained silent for the sake of party unity and in order to retain his hold on power and exert some influence on events as the international climate began to deteriorate. He acquiesced in 1936, when Hertzog amended the Constitution by further restricting the limited and indeed illusory franchise of the property-owning blacks in the Cape Province. When his brilliant younger colleague, Jan Hofmeyr,[53] voted with the minority against the amendment and in 1938 resigned from the Government in protest, Smuts commented, *I do not believe in the luxury of resignations, especially in times such as those through which we are passing ... The European situation*, he said with justice, *has got much worse.*[54]

Smuts and the Rise of Hitler

Far from being England's lackey, as his Afrikaner critics jeered, Smuts had fought successfully for the principle that sovereignty lay with Parliament in Cape Town and that the Commonwealth was *an alliance of free peoples.*[55] Thus in 1925, when Britain signed the Locarno Treaty, the Dominions at their request were exempted. The Balfour Declaration of 1926 recognised the Dominions as equal 'autonomous communities within the British Empire' and the Statute of Westminster in 1931 formally acknowledged their absolute right to determine their own domestic and foreign policy, including the issue of war and peace. As early as 1930, however, before the storm clouds once more loomed over Europe and while his hopes of the League of Nations were still high, Smuts made one thing clear. During a tour of America to plead the League's case, he soberly declared: *I am not a pacifist.* There were *greater things than peace*, he said, *ideals of justice, of fair play, of right, for which any decent human being ought to be prepared to give his life at any moment.*[56]

Smuts kept himself well-informed of events in Europe. He listened regularly to the radio news. He viewed the rise of Hitler, the resurgence of German nationalism and the persecution of the German Jews with abhorrence. During the First World War he had dismissed pan-German theories of a master-race as *arrant nonsense.*[57] *Would Luther or Goethe be tolerated in the Germany of today?*[58] he wrote to Arthur Gillett in 1934, finding Nazi Germany *even more repulsive*[59] than Bolshevik Russia. But he saw Nazism as a psychological consequence of the Treaty of Versailles, whose revision he continued to urge even as the threat from Germany increased. He justified in the name of fairness German demands for equal status with France and the right to rearm up to France's level. In a speech to the Royal Institute of International Affairs in 1934, he spoke of Germany's *inferiority complex*, for which the remedy was *to recognise her complete equality of status with her fellows.* He claimed that *the continuance of her Versailles status is becoming an offence to the conscience of Europe and a danger to future peace.*[60] For once, his faith in Germany and the belief that Nazism was a temporary aberration which fair play would put right, played him false. Three days later, Churchill, in a speech of robust common sense, pointedly asked whether the Nazis were the sort of people likely to sit calmly with Smuts 'and have their inferiority complex removed in friendly, reasonable debate?'[61] Smuts, however, continued to speak the language of appeasement to a worried and receptive public at the very time when Hitler, having withdrawn Germany from the League of Nations, was poised to launch his stated policy of destroying the Versailles Settlement piece by piece.

Smuts thought it a mistake to refuse to Nazi Germany what should have been conceded to Weimar Germany, as if there were no difference in the danger represented by the two regimes. *Repugnant as the principle of Nazism may be,* he argued, logically but perhaps unwisely, *that surely is no reason why Germany's equal international status should not be recognized?*[62] He wrote in 1935 of his desire to see Britain follow *a resolute policy of appeasement and reconstruction of the Peace.*[63] In the radically changed circumstances of the 1930s, the concept of 'appeasement' was mutating from the concessions from strength advocated by Smuts in 1919 into something very different: propitiation from weakness. Smuts even suggested colonial transfers to Germany, though not in South-West Africa or Tanganyika.

Smuts's attitude by 1938 was contradictory. On the one hand he seems to have appreciated the risks of appeasing Hitler. *A decent Germany,* he wrote in 1936, *might have been a good friend; it is difficult to think of Nazi Germany as safe company in future.*[64] He was appalled at Hitler's brutal take-over of Austria. Nazism was *Prussianism plus paganism*,[65] he declared. On the other hand, the Treaty of Versailles still remained in his eyes morally indefensible. He opposed any British guarantee to Czechoslovakia, since ostensibly at least the cause of the German minority there was just. He took the view that South Africa should fight only if Britain was threatened. In the Munich Crisis of September 1938, when war over Czechoslovakia seemed imminent, Hertzog, with Smuts's assent, announced South Africa's intention of remaining neutral. *I do not think a world war was justified over Czechoslovakia*,[66] Smuts wrote, but he noted realistically that Hitler had *tasted blood and his appetite may continue.*[67]

Hitler's occupation of Prague in March 1939 stripped the veil from his eyes. Hitler's latest coup was made vivid for Smuts by association with his visit 20 years before as an Emissary of the Peace Conference. *Hitler has made another of his stunning blows and another sovereign state lies prostrate before Germany*, he wrote. *Hitler sits today in the old Castle in Prague where I found Masaryk in April 1919.*[68] South Africa's official policy remained neutrality, but Smuts was taking no chances. On his own authority as Minister of Justice, he sent a police force into South-West Africa to forestall a possible pro-Nazi coup. He spoke often and publicly against the illusion that South Africa was safe from attack because of its remoteness from Europe. *We are a country worth conquering*, he pointed out. South Africa was dependant on the Royal Navy. Other than that, *we have not a ship to protect our shores.*[69]

Hitler's next demand was for Danzig and the Polish Corridor. By an ironic turn of fate, the German press cynically published Smuts's letter to Lloyd George of March 1919 in which he had protested against Danzig's severance from Germany. *It is pretty rotten*, he reflected, *to have my warnings of 20 years ago now twisted and used against us*; for as he clearly saw, if Germany did fight for Danzig, *Danzig will be merely the specious excuse.*[70] With the conclusion in August 1939 of the Nazi-Soviet Pact, a pact between *The Devil and Beelzebub*,[71] said Smuts, war in Europe was inevitable. The question was: what role would South Africa play? And what role Smuts himself?

9

Smuts and the Second World War: 1939–45

On 3 September 1939 Britain declared war on Germany. Thanks largely to Smuts's fight for constitutional sovereignty, South Africa was not bound as in 1914 by Britain's action, and was free to make her own choice. Hertzog was for neutrality, Smuts was adamant for war, a decision he described as the gravest he ever took in his life. The Cabinet was split down the middle: six were for Hertzog, seven for Smuts. The next day Hertzog introduced in the Assembly a motion in favour of neutrality. It so happened that the Assembly had been summoned that day to prolong the life of the Senate. But for this chance, Hertzog and not Parliament might have decided the question of war or peace. Just as in 1914, Hertzog made plain his pro-German sympathies.

Smuts moved an amendment to enter the war on Britain's side. Danzig, he repeated, was only the pretext for war. The real cause was Hitler's limitless ambition. He argued that without Commonwealth solidarity South Africa itself was vulnerable, not least from South-West Africa, long a hotbed of Nazism. Smuts's record of patience and loyalty in the

Hertzog coalition enhanced his credibility in the Assembly. On a free vote, his amendment was carried by 80 votes to 67, a majority of 13. It was enough. Rejecting Hertzog's advice to call a general election, the Governor-General invited Smuts to form a government. Hertzog resigned and the United Party split on the issue of participation in the war. Smuts became Prime Minister on 6 September at the age of 69. He remained in office until 1948.

As Prime Minister, Minister of Defence, Foreign Minister, and from June 1940 Commander-in-Chief of the Combined Forces of Southern Africa (including Rhodesia), Smuts took to the task with all his old zeal, energy and high good humour. He bounded upstairs to his office 'like a springbok'[1] while colleagues waited for the lift. He opened his first Cabinet meeting with the words: *Well, gentlemen, we must now declare war on Germany.*[2] He had always had the determination to enforce measures he thought necessary. He also had the skills to steer them through Parliament despite his initial slender majority, and he was scrupulous in respecting the democratic forms of the Constitution of which he was himself the author. Lithe, cheerful and alert, he was more than a match for the gruelling daily round, directing South Africa's military strategy and lending his ready counsels to the War Cabinet in London.

He immediately interned pro-Nazi agitators in South-West Africa. He kept a wary eye on subversive nationalist and pro-Nazi Afrikaner groups within South Africa itself bent on sabotaging the war effort, notably the *Ossewa Brandwag* (the Ox-Wagon Guard), a populist movement founded in 1938 to celebrate the centenary of the Great Trek, and the select and secretive *Broederbond* (the Brotherhood). The *Broederbond* and the *Ossewa Brandwag* numbered between them three future Prime Ministers of South Africa (Daniel-François Malan, Hendrik Verwoerd and Balthazar [BJ] Vorster), while Oswald Pirow, lately Minister of Defence, was an avowed Nazi. Towards such men Smuts was cautious and even indulgent: for unique among the Dominions, the opposition in South Africa was against the war, and he did not want another Jopie Fourie. His moderation proved wise and in 1943 he won a fresh mandate in a triumphant general election.

A regular speaker and broadcaster at home and in Britain, Smuts displayed the qualities that inspire confidence: poise, detachment, optimism, perspective and humour. He was, said the Governor-General, 'a great rock in a weary world'.[3] The day after Rommel's victory at Sidi Rezegh near Tobruk in November 1941, Smuts, standing 'perfectly serene and composed' in front of a large military map, explained the reasons for the defeat as if it were merely a matter of historical interest. 'It was a great disaster,' a listener recalled. 'It could have meant the loss of North Africa.' But 'hearing him explain with a smile on his eager face, there was no hint to me of despair or even of disaster. He was sure of ultimate victory. This was a minor setback. His hope, his faith and his optimism were supreme.'[4] In 1944, in the course of a visit to Commonwealth troops in Italy as they fought their way up the peninsula, Smuts found himself near Lake Trasimene, where the Carthaginian leader Hannibal had beaten the Romans in 217 BC. With the same sense of historical perspective, Smuts treated the officers to an off-the-cuff lecture on that battle of 2,000 years before.

Smuts retained in his seventies all his buoyant intrepidity. In 1940, the plane in which he was flying, a converted Junkers, was mistaken for an enemy aircraft, shot at and almost brought down. The fuselage was riddled with bullets, one of which had narrowly missed him. He made light of it. Twice on long-haul flights across Africa his plane was violently buffeted by tropical storms and struck by lightning. He never stirred. In London in 1944, he watched from his hotel window the first of Hitler's V1 flying bombs rain down on the capital as impassively as he had watched the German air-raids in the First World War.

His constitution was as strong as ever. He had never smoked, he drank little and he kept himself fit by his frugal habits and hard physical activity, including a weekly climb up Table Mountain when Parliament was sitting and strenuous walks at Doornkloof. As ever, Doornkloof was his refuge from the heavy responsibilities: *this blessed place*,[5] he called it, *full of small grandchildren and of abounding love*,[6] though one visitor described it as a 'tin hovel, crawling with screaming children and cluttered up with every sort of junk'.[7] His administrative burden was eased by Hofmeyr, now Finance Minister, who deputised for him during his frequent absences abroad.

South Africa was wholly unprepared for war. Smuts rapidly and energetically built up her land, sea and air defences. Volunteers – and as in the First World War, all were volunteers – flocked to the colours, some 200,000 in all. He sent his *boys*,[8] as he called them, north to Kenya and from there against the Italians in Ethiopia. They fought in all the North African campaigns, sharing in the massive Allied defeat at Tobruk, where 25,000 of the 32,000 Allied captives were South African, and in the victory at El Alamein in 1942. They fought in Sicily and Italy and their aircrews were conspicuous in operations with the Royal Air Force. With the Mediterranean under German and Italian control, the Cape route, as in 1914, increased South Africa's strategic importance until 1943. South Africans took part in the seizure of Madagascar from the Vichy French in 1942 to prevent its capture by the Japanese.

Smuts and Churchill

In the course of the war Smuts paid nine visits to Europe and the Middle East to confer with Allied leaders. He had long been a friend of Churchill. They had first met during the Boer War when Churchill, then a war correspondent, was captured and brought before him; and in after years they were always 'Winston' and 'Jan'. Throughout the Second World War Smuts was a fervent admirer of Churchill – *the one indispensable man.*[10] Smuts was one of the few whose advice Churchill respected, though he did not always follow it. In June 1940 Smuts urged him to throw all of Britain's air resources into the battle for France, one piece of advice which Churchill fortunately rejected. In February 1941, at the promptings of Smuts as well as of Churchill, Archibald Wavell began the invasion of Italian Somaliland which led to the rapid conquest of Ethiopia and Eritrea and the end of Mussolini's African Empire. Later the same year Smuts was promoted to the rank of Field Marshal in the British army, though his critics saw this as further proof that he had sold out to the British, and he always preferred to be known as 'General Smuts'.

'His integrity was beyond question and his directness almost a legend. When he addressed us – the boys – before we went up North in the last War he said (and I remember it so well): *Some of you will not come back. Some of you will come back maimed. Those of you who do come back will come back changed men. That is war!* And "his boys" cheered him.'

SIR DAVID DE VILLIERS GRAAFF[9]

'He stands out head and shoulders above any other person here [in London]. His pre-eminence as a statesman no one has disputed, and I hear it daily confirmed with greater emphasis. To people he is both a tonic and an elixir. He is also a symbol of steadfastness and security, and the embodiment of optimism and the higher values of life ... He cuts a very handsome and inspiring figure on the public platform, dressed in his military uniform ... His face looks so strong and handsome, with its healthy, rosy colouring, his blue eyes, his trim white beard and snowy hair. When he talks, his face lights up with expression, and you cannot help being infected with his goodwill and sincerity.'

JAN SMUTS JUNIOR ON HIS FATHER, AUTUMN 1943[11]

Smuts was often at Churchill's side. 'He really cares for Winston,' wrote Churchill's wife, 'and is the source of strength and encouragement to him.'[12] He was with Churchill in Cairo in 1942, when he urged Claude Auchinleck's replacement as commander in the desert war, and subsequently General Bernard Montgomery's appointment as commander of the Eighth Army. He joined Churchill in Downing Street, at Chequers and in 1944 in the south of England on the eve of D-Day; and he accompanied him to France after the Normandy landings. He took part in meetings of the War Cabinet and Churchill wanted to appoint him acting Prime Minister during his absence at Teheran in 1943.'My faith in Smuts is unbreakable,'[13] he declared. It was even suggested that if Churchill died, Smuts should replace him as Prime Minister. As in the First World War, Smuts had firm views on strategy. His conviction of the need to clear the enemy from North Africa and the Mediterranean was vindicated at

El Alamein; and he strongly supported 'Operation Torch', the Anglo-American landings in Morocco and Algeria and the subsequent advance into Sicily and Italy in 1942 and 1943.

In both World Wars Smuts was an inspirational leader and a cool calculator, who based his decisions on *brute hard facts*.[14] He detested war but once convinced there was no alternative, faced it squarely. Of his advice on the projected Passchendaele campaign in 1917, his son noted 'how cool and resolute he could be provided he felt the end justified the means. Not many men would have been able to write with a steady hand: *Losses at 100,000 a month=less than half a million, whom we can make good*'.[15] In the Second World War he strongly supported the bombing of German cities, the policy he had recommended in World War I; and its chief protagonist, Air Chief Marshal Sir Arthur 'Bomber' Harris, who, wrote Smuts's son, 'had no weightier champion than my father'.[16] Sir Alan Lascelles, private secretary to King George VI, recorded a bishop saying that 'greatly as he admired Smuts, he considered him a very callous man. He is passionately interested in the battle between Good and Evil, but not at all in how many people are killed.' Lascelles commented, 'In other words, he takes a sternly objective view of the war, as, I should say, every successful statesman must of any human problem. But I don't think that necessarily implies callousness.'[17]

Smuts was concerned, however, at the risks of Operation 'Overlord', the Normandy landings, and Operation 'Anvil' – the landings in the south of France. He preferred a concerted advance through Italy and the Balkans. When Churchill, who had pledged himself on Overlord to Roosevelt and Stalin, proved unresponsive, Smuts tried enlisting the Chiefs of Staff and even King George VI, who wrote urging Churchill to reconsider, but to no avail. Churchill described his relationship with Smuts as that of 'two old love-birds moulting together on a perch but still able to peck'.[18]

As in the First World War, Smuts, through his public appearances and now his broadcasts, was an amazingly popular figure in Britain. The wife of the British High Commissioner in South Africa wrote in 1942, 'He does give one a greater feeling of security and poise than almost everyone I've ever met.'[19] In 1942 he addressed both Houses of Parliament in a broadcast speech. An observer noted, 'His style is simple and incisive, and he conveys an impression of the great wisdom that he undoubtedly has.'[20] In this address Smuts viewed the Second World War in its historical perspective as a continuation of the First, and the whole period since 1914 as *another Thirty Years War ... interrupted by an armistice in 1919 improperly called a peace.*[21] A year later, in another speech in London, he reflected on the failure of the League of Nations to deter Hitler and Mussolini. The lesson, he said, was that *peace unbacked by power remains a dream.* Unless *this fundamental factor* was taken into account, *all our idealism, all our high aspirations for a better world*[23] were in vain.

By 1944 Smuts had become alarmed by the growing threat

'... old Smuts, sitting like an owl on its perch, would hop down and play an always predominant part. At one moment he set out, with his blue eyes flashing and his beard all a-twitch, to expound to us his favourite philosophy of holism, based, I understand, on the paradox that the whole is *not* the sum of, but is greater than, its component parts. It is certainly true enough of the British Empire.'
SIR ALAN LASCELLES, PRIVATE SECRETARY TO KING GEORGE VI, DIARY, 20 OCTOBER 1943[22]

posed to Europe by a victorious Russia. His qualms stemmed from his own experience of over-mighty nations. Russia had become a *Colossus*, he wrote to Margaret Gillett. *How will she use her immense power and unprecedented position when the war is over?*[24] A year later, with Russia *mistress of the Continent*, he wrote, *I know how dangerous the predominance of any one Power can be, and how liable such dominant power is to abuse. I remember British jingoism and the Boer War, and I know Russia has even less experience and human wisdom than the British.*[25] As for Germany, with her defeat imminent, Smuts was asked what Allied policy towards her would be. He replied with the same characteristic generosity as he had shown in November 1918 that while war criminals would be brought to book, *I cannot see us standing by while the population starve. You will find that humanitarianism will prevail and we will help them again on to their feet.*[26]

10
'Superhuman Courage': Smuts 1945–50

In 1945, Smuts headed a victorious South Africa: a young country industrialised, enriched by the war and attractive to investors and immigrants. As ever looking to the future, he asked, *What is to become of Europe?*[1] In San Francisco to participate in the foundation of the United Nations, successor to the League, Smuts was given pride of place as what Britain's Foreign Secretary, Anthony Eden, called the 'doyen of the Conference – quite unrivalled in intellectual attributes and unsurpassed in experience and authority'.[2] It was Smuts who drafted the preamble to the United Nations Charter, including a declaration of *fundamental human rights*. He called it *a statement of faith – the things we stand for.*[3]

As the war against Hitler came to an end and the Cold War began to emerge, Smuts witnessed the ominous acrimonious exchanges between the three Great Powers (Russia, and America and Britain). *But Paul's Three – the real Big Three*, he wrote (faith, hope and charity), *I see little of.*[5] In 1946 he was in London and Paris, attending the second Paris Peace Conference as South Africa's representative 25 years after the first. He 'conveys the impression of a philosopher-king,' wrote Harold Nicolson, 'very old, very wise.' Smuts counselled patience over the Cold War. 'He says that those who contend that time is ... not a creative factor are denying all experience. There are situations in which time is the only solvent. *We should play for time – time at any cost, time in any form*.'[6]

Smuts's enduring belief was in the primacy of moral principle and right conduct in international relations. He gave an instance of how this had worked during the Second World War with the decision taken by Churchill on the advice of Wavell and Smuts in Spring 1941 to go to the assistance of Greece, even though they knew it must end in defeat. *But we made our decision, not on military principles, but on moral principles*, he said. Intervention in Greece served to delay Hitler's invasion of Russia by six weeks, fatal for Germany. *She lost time – and with time she lost Moscow, Stalingrad and the war ... This shows once again that to do the right thing is generally the right thing to do.*[7] Ever faithful to the Balfour Declaration and his friendship for the Jews, Smuts recognized the State of Israel in 1948 long before Britain or any other Commonwealth country. Yet there was an unresolved tension in Smuts between his basic optimism and confidence in an

> **THE ORDER OF THE MAN OF GALILEE**
> During the Second World War, when the Allies were again discussing a post-war New World Order, Smuts said *We do not want new orders. What the world wants is an old order of 2,000 years ago – the order of the Man of Galilee.* While in 1945 he drafted the preamble to the Charter of the United Nations, with its emphasis on *fundamental human rights*. He later confided, *I find our modern emphasis on 'rights' somewhat overdone and misleading ... It makes people forget that the other and more important side of rights is duty. And indeed the great historic codes of our human advance emphasised duties and not rights ... The Ten Commandments in the Old Testament and ... the Sermon on the Mount ... all are silent on rights, all lay stress on duties.*[5]

orderly universe reflected in *Holism and Evolution* and his awareness of *the power of chaos* which he had seen *at the heart of things*[8] at Paris.

Though he loathed Nazism as a scourge that must be beaten, Smuts always felt greater affinity for Germany than for France. Just as after the Boer War he retained his faith in *that other England*[10] which he knew from his Cambridge days, so he never ceased to hold 'that other Germany' in the highest regard. *I looked on the Germans*, he said, *as the most cultivated race in the world. The French hated me for my belief in them.*[11] *One longs ardently*, he reflected in *the sad and cruel times* of Hitler, *for the return of those great days when the German spirit was voiced by Goethe and Schiller and Kant.*[12] French culture seems to have passed him by and to have played little or no part in his intellectual make-up. He told King George VI in 1942, *We can never trust the French, for they can never forget that they were masters of Europe for 200 years.*[13] The following year, in a speech to members of both Houses of Parliament which he had wrongly been told would be a closed meeting, he said that France was finished as a Great Power. The Nazis quickly circulated the speech in France.

True, at the start of the war, he had confided, *I have left off*

WHAT WOULD HE HAVE DONE? Throughout his long friendship with the Clark family, and particularly during the two World Wars, Smuts strove to confront the challenge of their Quaker pacifism. *I do believe that under ideal conditions the Christian message is the only answer to our difficulties,* Smuts wrote to Margaret Gillett on 7 June 1942. *But of course the situation for Jesus was much simplified by the existence of the omnipotent Roman Empire and by his sound principle of leaving to Caesar what was Caesars's. We, on the other hand, are in the position of Caesar, responsible for peace and war, for the maintenance of a social order against brute violence and aggression. Ours therefore is a much more complex situation than that which Jesus had to face. What would He have done if in Caesar's place?*[9]

being soft about Germany, describing Germany as *the per-petual ruin of Europe*[14] and *the enemy of the human race*,[15] and said that after the war *Germany will have to be broken up into what she was before 1870*.[16] But his ingrained affection for Germany resurfaced. By the end of the war he had reverted to his former views. *I don't hate Germans*, he wrote to Margaret Gillett, *and I feel deeply for Europe of which Germany remains an integral, if not a dominant part*.[17] When he learned that his old First World War adversary and friend, von Lettow-Vorbeck, had fallen on hard times, he sent him food parcels and arranged for a pension to be paid to him.

For Smuts, Europe was always the centre of civilisation, and the two European peoples in South Africa, Boer and British, were the guardians of civilisation there. Towards the majority population, despite occasional statements to the contrary, including a proposal, which outraged his opponents, to arm the blacks if South Africa were invaded, he held throughout his career to the traditional Afrikaner prejudice, and confirmed that, as he told Parliament in 1945, *it is a fixed policy to maintain white supremacy in South Africa*.[18] Under his successor, Malan, the system of 'apartheid' or 'separate development' was formalised by the Nationalists, who remained in office until 1994 and took South Africa out of the Commonwealth from 1961 to 1994.

When in 1919 Smuts secured a League of Nations Mandate for South-West Africa, it had been in the belief that this was *annexation in all but name*.[19] Just over a quarter of a century later, post-war decolonialisation and the rise of the 'Third World', represented by an independent India long aggrieved at Smuts's treatment of South Africa's Indian minority, defeated his expectations. In 1946 he appeared in person before the United Nations to seek the termination of the

Mandate and the incorporation of South-West Africa within the Union. His presence was a mark of his respect, as a jurist, constitutionalist and internationalist, for the principles of international law. He might, after all, as W K Hancock points out, have simply annexed the territory with impunity. But the United Nations proved no improvement on the League. At India's instigation, the General Assembly rejected incorporation by 37 votes to nine. Smuts lamented its partisan fatuity – another *talking shop in which incompetents and misfits rule by counting of heads.*[20] It was *a bitter experience*[21] for Smuts and a severe blow to his prestige.

Towards the end of his life Smuts thought about how, if he remained in power, as he expected, education and democracy might best be extended to the majority. *How is the practical compromise to be found?* he pondered. *That is the problem which confronts us in South Africa and me in particular ... And in South Africa the problem is coming to a head.* He was well aware of the irony of his position and of what would be said of him: *Here is the author of the great Preamble of the Charter, exposed as a hypocrite and a double-faced time-server!*[22] His friend Theo Haarhof was convinced that the logic of holism would have led Smuts to a still greater level of humanity, more inclusive and complete. It is hard to think of Smuts not warming to Nelson Mandela as a kindred spirit: like Smuts, purged of bitterness in the *fires of adversity*,[23] his inauguration as President – 'the time for the healing of the wounds'. Mandela wrote magnanimously of Smuts: 'I cared more that he had helped the foundation of the League of Nations, promoting freedom throughout the world, than the fact that he had repressed freedom at home.'[24] Statues of both men now adorn London's Parliament Square. At the time, however, Smuts saw no alternative to separate development, and his attitude from 1906 onwards was *to shift the intolerable burden of solving that sphinx problem to the ampler shoulders and stronger brains of the future.*[25]

Smuts after the war was as active and blithe as ever. In 1947 he entertained with gusto the British King and Queen and the Royal Princesses in South Africa. To a colleague who urged him to stay on in London after a visit later that year, he said, *No, no, my boy. I must get back. While I'm away none of my Ministers make decisions.*[26] But heavy blows soon fell on him in his old age. First the shock of losing the election in May 1948. He had planned a golden future for South Africa as the industrial centre of the continent, prosperous and liberal. He won a majority of votes, but not of seats and lost the election thanks to his own insistence when drafting the Constitution in 1909 on giving greater weight to votes in rural constituencies. *My Boers have turned from me,*[27] he reflected. They had indeed turned against him, assisted by the Germans of South-West Africa. He even lost his own seat in the Transvaal. For a time he felt crushed – *crucified,*[28] he said. He decided nonetheless to stay on as leader of the opposition and was able to joke about his fall from power. To Churchill, also smarting from electoral defeat, he said, *It's good for us old fogeys to be kicked out!*[29] He was gratified to be installed as Chancellor of Cambridge University but was again badly shaken in October by the sudden death of his eldest son, Japie, followed in December by that of Jan Hofmeyr, whom he had looked on as the future leader of his party.

So many of his hopes had come to nothing: hopes of a Greater South Africa – the recognised frontiers of the Union in 1950 were just as they had been in 1910; and hopes for peace and goodwill in the world – the Peace Conference of 1919 had sown the seeds of a second world conflict which the League of Nations had failed to prevent. The Cold War boded ill and the United Nations looked even less promising than the League. Smuts never wholly succeeded in healing the rift between Afrikaner and Briton in South Africa and to many on both sides he always remained suspect. 'If it were not his creed to hope,' wrote his biographer Sarah Millin, 'he might despair.'[30] Steeped in ancient history, Smuts often looked back on the great Carthaginian general Hannibal and his wars with Rome which ended in defeat. He was haunted by a description of Hannibal by the German historian Theodor Mommsen: 'On those whom the gods love they lavish infinite joys and infinite sorrows.'[31]

But the indomitable Smuts dug within himself and still found deep reserves of fortitude and optimism. Stricken with back pain, pain of a degree he had never experienced in his life, he thought it *good policy to keep up appearances. In looking cheerful you make others cheerful and end up by really feeling cheered up yourself.*[32] A colleague saw him leaning against a door-post for support, for the pain was too great for him to stand upright, 'Yet standing there he was the picture of the happiest, kindliest, friendliest being on earth.' [33] Sarah Millin was moved to express to him her admiration for 'your greatness and courage, your superhuman courage'.[34] There was no abatement of his holistic idealism, his goodwill, his magnanimity. One of his last speeches, delivered on his 80th birthday on 24 May 1950, was a plea to the West to treat Germany as an equal. The same day he suffered the first of a succession of heart attacks. He struggled on.

Smuts had always wanted to write a study of South African flora, a life of Kruger and a revised edition of *Holism and Evolution*. In July a visitor to his bedside suggested that he devote his convalescence to the latter. *No*, he replied. *I must go on working for my own country until the end of my life.*[35] Two months later, on 11 September 1950, Jan Christian Smuts died in his simple iron bedstead at Doornkloof. His Greek New Testament and the poems of Emily Brontë were on his bedside table. 'He looked so happy in death,' wrote his daughter, 'with just a suggestion of a smile on his face.'[36] The Government gave him a state military funeral in Pretoria, but his remains were brought back to Doornkloof. 'Here, in this picturesque corner of our sunny veld,' wrote his son, 'we scattered his ashes.'[37]

Conclusion

'For famous men the whole earth is their monument.'
                                                    THUCYDIDES

'Jan Smuts did not belong to any single state or nation. He fought for his own country, he thought for the whole world.'
          WINSTON CHURCHILL, IN THE HOUSE OF COMMONS, 26 JUNE 1952

Smuts's experience of *political magnanimity* – the hand of friendship extended by Britain's Liberal government in 1906 to the vanquished Boer Republics – inspired his thoughts and feelings about international relations for the rest of his life. With an optimism also born of his philosophy of holism, he masterminded the coalescence of the four former British colonies, to create in 1910 the Union of South Africa as a self-governing Dominion in the British Commonwealth of Nations (as he renamed the Empire); and he was, no less than Woodrow Wilson, the prophet of a *new world order* inaugurated by the League of Nations.

The Peace Conference of 1919 gave the Union of South Africa an independent voice in world affairs; though the voice, that of Smuts, was too little heeded where it counted most, in peacemaking with Germany. Through the signatures of

Botha and Smuts, South Africa's founding fathers and Plenipotentiaries, the Treaty of Versailles gave the seal of international recognition to the Union. It was with this imperative
and overriding end in mind, and impelled by an inescapable
sense of patriotic duty as his country's second representative, that Smuts overcame his deep repugnance to signing the
Treaty of which he so radically disapproved.

The Peace Conference mocked his hopes and ideals. No one
fought more earnestly or persistently for a peace of *appeasement* (in its original sense of concession from strength), as he
saw to his dismay the *bedrock* of a *Wilson peace* chipped away
by *the old policy of grab and greed and partitions*, ending in
a *Diktat* crammed with irritants. By a bitter irony, moreover,
Smuts, the man of principle and integrity who insisted that
the Allies must stick to their solemn contractual undertakings
enshrined in the Pre-Armistice Agreement, laid himself open
to criticism by his tenacious demands for the annexation of
German South-West Africa in the guise of a 'Mandate'; and
still more for his controversial legal opinion on the inclusion of military pensions in the reparations demanded of
Germany. His Boer enemies, who always saw him as a turn-
coat and British hireling, pointed knowingly to 'Slim Jannie'
and his sleight of hand.

Through the establishment of the League of Nations, the
great ordeal of the War seemed to Smuts to have brought
closer the millenarian hope of peace among the nations,
though even he sometimes wondered whether his faith in
the League might be a mirage. *I have spent much of my real
life*, he admitted, *in imaginary air castles*.[1] Clemenceau had
already voiced this doubt. 'Do you really believe it,' he asked,
'a peaceful world founded on violence?'[2]

Yet Smuts, in Churchill's words, remains 'one of the most

enlightened, courageous and noble-minded men of the twentieth century';[3] and the principle of goodwill and good faith which he upheld at Paris and after, his pervasive belief in *reconciliation* and *the contagion of magnanimity* live on in South Africa in men like Nelson Mandela and Archbishop Desmond Tutu. There is a Jan Smuts House at the Universities of Cape Town and Witwatersrand, and a Smuts Chair of International Relations at both, as well as of Commonwealth History at Cambridge. Neither in South Africa nor in Britain, however, are there any known plans to commemorate in 2010 the anniversaries of his birth or death. The simple house at Doornkloof remains a fitting monument to his greatness.

Notes

Preface and Acknowledgements

1. Smuts to Arthur Gillett, 12 January 1919, W K Hancock and J Van der Poel (ed) *Selections from the Smuts Papers,* 7 volumes (Cambridge University Press, Cambridge: 1966–1973), Vol 4, p 41, hereafter *SP.*

2. J Bainville, *Les conséquences politiques de la paix* (éditions de l'Arsenal, Paris: 1995), p 25.

3. G Martel, 'O what an ugly peace' (review of M Boemeke, G Feldman and Elisabeth Glaser [ed], *The Treaty of Versailles. A Reassessment after 75 Years* [Cambridge University Press, Cambridge: 1998], hereafter *Reassessment*), H-Diplo. Roundtable, 2 March 2001.

4. See W R Keylor, 'Versailles and International Diplomacy', in *Reassessment,* pp 469–505; M Fry, 'British Revisionism', in *Reassessment,* pp 565–601; and Zara Steiner, 'The Treaty of Versailles Revisited', in M Dockrill and J Fisher (ed), *The Paris Peace Conference, 1919. Peace without Victory?* (Palgrove in association with the Public Record Office, Basingstoke: 2001) pp 13–33.

5. *The New York Times,* 3 March 1921.

6. Smuts, Speech to American Editors, 14 November 1918, *SP*, Vol. 4, p 15.

7. *The New York Times,* 3 March 1921.

8. Smuts to Margaret Gillett, 27 December 1918, *SP*, Vol. 4, p 34. The emphasis is Smuts's.

9. Smuts, Rectorial Address at St Andrews University, 17 October 1934, J C Smuts, *Jan Christian Smuts* (Cassell, London: 1952) p 352, hereafter *JCS*.

10. *The Times,* 12 September 1950.

11. Smuts to Sarah Millin, April/May 1934, in Sarah G Millin, *The Measure of My Days* (Faber and Faber, London: 1955) p 124.

12. See Ronald Hyam, 'South Africa, Cambridge, and Commonwealth History', *The Round Table* (2001) Volume 90 360, pp 401–14.

13. P Beukes, *The Holistic Smuts. A Study in Personality* (Human and Rousseau, Cape Town: 1989) p 95, hereafter *Holistic Smuts*.

14. Harold Nicolson, *Peacemaking 1919* (Constable, London: 1933) p 37.

15. P B Blankenberg, *The Thoughts of General Smuts. Compiled by his Private Secretary* (Juta and Co, Cape Town: 1951) p 151, hereafter Blankenberg, *Thoughts*.

16. *The New York Times,* 3 March 1921.

17. Smuts to Margaret Gillett, 16 May 1919, *SP*, Vol. 4, p 162.

18. Wilson to Smuts, 9 February 1921, A S Link and others (ed), *The Papers of Woodrow Wilson* (Princeton University Press, Princeton, NJ: 1992) Vol. 67, pp 125–6, hereafter *PWW*.

19. See A Lentin, *Guilt at Versailles. Lloyd George and the Pre-History of Appeasement* (Methuen, London: 1985); and 'The Worm in the Bud: "Appeasement" at the Peace Conference', in A Lentin, *Lloyd George and the Lost Peace. From Versailles to Hitler, 1919–1940* (Palgrave, London: 2001) pp 67–88.

Prelude: 'I have fought and worked for a different peace'

1. 'Minutes of a Meeting of the British Empire Delegation', 1 June 1919, *British Documents on Foreign Affairs. Reports and Papers from the Foreign Office Confidential Prints*, K Bourne and D C Watt (ed), Part 2, Series 1, *The Paris Peace Conference of 1919*, M Dockrill (ed), vol. 4, *British Empire Delegation Minutes* (University Publications of America, Bethesda, MD: 1989) p 106, hereafter *BDFA*.
2. Smuts, Press Statement (1923), *SP*, Vol. 5, p 94.
3. *BDFA*, p 98.
4. *BDFA*, p 98.
5. *BDFA*, p 99.
6. Smuts to Margaret Gillett, 2 June 1919, *SP*, Vol. 4, p 212.
7. Smuts to Margaret Gillett, 23 June 1919, *SP*, Vol. 4, p 244.
8. Smuts to Margaret Gillett, 28 June 1919, *SP*, Vol. 4, pp 255, 256.
9. Smuts to Margaret Gillett, 30 December 1919, *SP*, Vol. 5, p 31.
10. T Wilson (ed), *The Political Diaries of C P Scott 1911–1928* (Collins, London: 1970) p 375, hereafter *Scott*.
11. Sarah G Millin, *General Smuts*, 2 volumes (Faber and Faber, London: 1936), Vol. 2, p 189, hereafter *GS*.
12. Smuts to Isie Smuts, 10 June 1919, *SP*, Vol. 4, p 225.

13. Smuts to C P Scott, 26 June 1919, *Scott*, p 375.
14. *GS*, Vol. 1, p 77.

1: Smuts – Scholar, Statesman, Soldier: 1870–1914

1. K A Keppel-Jones, *South Africa. A Short History* 5th edition (Hutchinson, London: 1982) p 75.
2. Sarah Millin, *The People of South Africa* (Constable, London: 1951) p 77, hereafter Millin, *People*.
3. *JCS*, p 21.
4. W K Hancock, *Smuts*, vol. 1, *The Sanguine Years 1870–1919* (Cambridge University Press, Cambridge: 1962) p 7, hereafter *Smuts Sanguine*.
5. *Scott*, p 284.
6. *GS*, Vol. 1, p 56.
7. One of his adolescent charges was his successor as Prime Minister in 1948, Daniel-François Malan.
8. *JCS*, p 18.
9. *JCS*, p 21.
10. *Walt Whitman* was published in 1973 by Wayne State University Press.
11. *Smuts Sanguine*, p 48.
12. *Smuts Sanguine*, p 55.
13. *JCS*, p 35.
14. Smuts, *Memoirs of the Boer War*, Gail Nattrass and S.B. Spiess (ed), (Jonathan Bull Publishers, Johannesburg: 1994) p 131, hereafter *Boer Memoirs*.
15. *Smuts Sanguine*, p 69.
16. *Smuts Sanguine*, p 69.
17. *JSC*, p 46.
18. *Smuts Sanguine*, p 95.
19. *A Century of Wrong*, in *Smuts Sanguine*, p 110.
20. *JCS*, p 49.

21. *Boer Memoirs,* p 48.
22. *Boer Memoirs,* p 39.
23. *Smuts Sanguine,* p 140.
24. *JCS,* p 24.
25. Smuts to Isie, 2 June 1901, *Smuts Sanguine,* p 131.
26. *Smuts Sanguine,* p 138.
27. D Reitz, *Commando. A Boer Journal of the Boer War* (Faber and Faber, London: 1935) p 208.
28. *JCS,* p 71.
29. *JCS,* p 78.
30. *Smuts Sanguine,* p 137.
31. Smuts to Adolf Meyer-Abich, 1948, in *Holistic Smuts,* p 205.
32. Reitz, *Commando,* p 289.
33. *Boer Memoirs,* p 151. By 'the common humanity which knows no "racial distinctions"', Smuts had in mind fellow-whites, the British and Dominion troops of European descent. His attitude to South Africa's majority black population was paternalistic but did not extend to political or social equality. Blacks would be excluded from citizenship in the Union of South Africa.
34. *GS,* Vol. 1, p 138.
35. Emily Hobhouse to Smuts, 29 May 1904, in P Beukes, *The Romantic Smuts. Women and Love in his Life* (Human and Rousseau, Cape Town: 1992) p 47, hereafter *Romantic Smuts.*
36. P Beukes, *The Religious Smuts* (Human and Rousseau, Cape Town: 1994) p 32, hereafter *Religious Smuts.*
37. *JCS,* p 82.
38. *Smuts Sanguine,* p 164.
39. *GS,* Vol. 1, p 182.
40. *Romantic Smuts,* p 51.

41. *Smuts Sanguine,* Vol. 1, p 168.
42. Smuts to Emily Hobhouse, 8 May 1904, in *Romantic Smuts,* p 45.
43. *JCS,* p 95.
44. Smuts to Emily Hobhouse, 21 February 1904, in *Holistic Smuts,* p 49.
45. Smuts, 1929, in *Holistic Smuts,* p 68.
46. Smuts, 1929, in *Holistic Smuts,* p 67.
47. Smuts, 1929, in *Holistic Smuts,* p 68.
48. Smuts, 1905, in *Holistic Smuts,* p 89.
49. E.g. Smuts to Isie Smuts, 26 September 1916, *SP,* Vol. 3, p 405.
50. Smuts, Speech at Botha's Funeral, 30 August 1919, *SP,* Vol. 4, p 288.
51. *Smuts Sanguine,* p 198.
52. *GS,* Vol 1, p 212.
53. *Romantic Smuts,* p 51.
54. *Romantic Smuts,* p 63.
55. *Smuts Sanguine,* p 215.
56. *Smuts Sanguine,* p 215.
57. Lord Riddell, Diary, 27 April 1913, in J M McEwen (ed), *The Riddell Diaries 1908–1923* (Athlone Press, London: 1986) p 63.
58. *Religious Smuts,* p 94.
59. *Religious Smuts,* p 96.
60. *JCS,* pp 98–9.
61. Smuts, Speech to American Editors, 14 November 1918, *SP,* Vol. 4, p 16.
62. *People,* p 129.
63. W K Hancock, *Smuts,* vol. 2, *The Fields of Force 1919–1950* (Cambridge University Press, Cambridge: 1968) p 495, hereafter *Smuts Force.*

64. L Egeland, 'Counsellor of Kings', in Zelda Friedlander (ed), *Jan Smuts Remembered: A Centennial Tribute* (Allan Wingate, London: 1970) p 33.

65. *GS,* Vol. 1, p 261.

66. *Smuts Sanguine,* p 235.

67. *Smuts Sanguine,* p 235.

68. Millin, *People,* p 117.

69. *JCS,* p 271.

70. W Busschau, in Friedlander, *Jan Smuts Remembered,* p 27.

71. (Lady) Daphne Moore, Diary, 31 January 1943, in *Romantic Smuts,* pp 128–9.

72. *JCS,* p 268.

73. Blankenberg, *Thoughts,* p 189.

74. T J Haarhof, *Smuts the Humanist: A Personal Reminiscence* (Blackwell, Oxford: 1970) p 34.

75. Smuts to Adolf Meyer-Abich, July 1948, in *Holistic Smuts,* p 205.

76. Smuts, Speech, 25 February 1923, in *Holistic Smuts,* p 49.

77. Smuts to J A Hobson, in *Smuts Sanguine,* p 255.

78. *Smuts Sanguine,* p 369.

79. *Smuts Sanguine,* pp 346–7.

80. *GS,* Vol 1, pp 287–8.

2: War and Peace: 1914–18

1. 30 July 1914, in *Smuts Sanguine,* p 374.

2. *Smuts Sanguine,* p 378.

3. C A W Manning, '"Empire" into "Commonwealth"', in G A Panichas (ed), *Promise of Greatness. The War of 1914–1918* (Cassell, London: 1968) p 428.

4. Smuts to Arthur Gillett, 27 September 1914, in *Smuts Sanguine*, p 378.

5. *Smuts Sanguine*, p 383.

6. *GS*, Vol. 1, p 165.

7. *GS*, Vol. 1, p 332.

8. Smuts to Margaret Gillett, 1916, in *Holistic Smuts*, p 173.

9. *Smuts Sanguine*, p 406.

10. *Smuts Sanguine*, p 407.

11. *JCS*, p 165.

12. Smuts to Margaret Gillett, 2 May 1916, in *Smuts Sanguine*, p 415.

13. Blankenberg, *Thoughts*, p 177; *JCS*, p 170.

14. F Brett Young, in *JCS*, p 175.

15. F Owen, *Tempestuous Journey. Lloyd George, His Life and Times* (Hutchinson, London: 1954) p 307.

16. *Holistic Smuts*, p 91.

17. Lord Riddell, Diary, 18 May 1917, in J M McEwen (ed), *The Riddell Diaries*, p 189.

18. L S Amery, *My Political Life*, Vol. 2, *War and Peace 1914–1929* (Hutchinson, London: 1953) p 99.

19. *Scott*, p 286.

20. Lord Shaw of Dunfermline, *Letters to Isabel* (George H Doran Co, New York: 1921) p 202. The case on which Lord Shaw sat was *R v Halliday, ex parte Zadig* (1917).

21. *JCS*, p 179.

22. Smuts to Isie Smuts, *SP*, 1917, Vol. 3, p 474.

23. *Smuts Sanguine*, p 429.

24. *Scott*, p 284.

25. Smuts to Margaret Gillett, 17 December 1918, *SP*, Vol. 4, p 28.

26. C Weizmann, *Trial and Error* (Hamish Hamilton, London: 1949) p 203.

27. Colonel R Meinertzhagen, in *Smuts Sanguine,* p 412.

28. *Scott,* p 306.

29. Smuts to Margaret Gillett, 20 July 1919, *SP,* Vol. 4, p 276.

30. *Smuts Sanguine,* p 438.

31. Smuts to Wolstenholme, 6 August 1917, *JCS,* p 197.

32. *Holistic Smuts,* p 174.

33. Smuts, Speech, 14 May 1917, *JCS,* p 211.

34. *JCS,* p 211.

35. Smuts, *War-Time Speeches* (Hodder and Stoughton, London: 1917) p 57.

36. Smuts, *War-Time Speeches,* p 58.

37. Smuts, Speech, 14 May 1917, *JCS,* p 212.

38. F S Oliver, 1917, *JCS,* p 187.

39. Smuts, Memorandum, 'The General Strategic and Military Situation', 29 April 1917, in D Lloyd George, *War Memoirs,* 2 volumes (Odham, London: 1938) Vol. 1, p 910.

40. 'Imperial War Cabinet Committee on Territorial Desiderata', 17 April 1917, W R Louis, *Great Britain and Germany's Lost Colonies 1914–1919* (Oxford University Press, Oxford: 1967) p 82.

41. Louis, *Great Britain and Germany's Lost Colonies*, p 82.

42. Lloyd George, *War Memoirs,* Vol. 1, p 913.

43. *JCS,* p 200.

44. C Addison, Diary, 1 January 1918, in J Grigg, *Lloyd George. War Leader 1916–1918* (Allen Lane, London: 2002) p 378.

45. Smuts to Isie Smuts, 27 April 1917, *SP,* Vol. 3, p 482.

46. *JCS,* p 187.

47. Smuts to Lloyd George, 13 April 1918, in Lord Beaverbrook, *Men and Power 1917–1918* (Hutchinson, London: 1956) p 223.

48. *Smuts Sanguine,* p 483.

49. Scott, Diary, 20 March 1918, in *Scott,* p 337.

50. *Holistic Smuts,* p 36.

51. Scott, Diary, 20–21 March 1918, in *Scott,* p 338.

52. G Dangerfield, *The Damnable Question. A Study in Anglo-Irish Relations* (Quartet Books, London: 1979) pp 291, 277; Thomas Jones, Diary, 9 May 1918, K Middlemas (ed), *Whitehall Diary* (Oxford University Press, Oxford, 1969) Vol. 1, p 63.

53. C Addison, *Politics from Within 1911–1918* (Herbert Jenkins, London: 1924) p 265.

54. *JCS,* p 207.

55. *JCS,* p 209.

56. Smuts, 'A note on the early conclusion of peace, October 24, 1918', quoted by D French in *Reassessment,* p 79.

57. Smuts to Alice Clark, 1 April 1919, *SP,* Vol. 4, p 100.

58. Smuts, Memorandum, 24 October 1918, in Lloyd George, *War Memoirs,* Vol. 2, p 1973.

59. Lloyd George, *War Memoirs,* Vol. 2, p 1973.

60. Lloyd George, *War Memoirs,* Vol. 2, p 1973.

61. Smuts, 'A note on the early conclusion of peace, October 24, 1918', in *Reassessment,* p 79.

62. Smuts, 26 October 1918, in R E Bunselmeyer, *The Costs of the War 1914–1919* (Archon Books, Hamden, CT: 1975) p 80.

63. *Smuts Sanguine,* p 495.

64. Smuts, Speech to American Editors, 14 November 1918, *SP,* Vol. 4, p 12.

65. Smuts to Arthur Gillett, 10 November 1918, in *Romantic Smuts,* pp 102–3.

3: Peacemaking: November 1918–February 1919

1. Addison, *Politics from Within 1911–1918,* p 265.
2. Smuts, 'Our Policy at the Peace Conference', 3 December 1918, National Archives, Foreign Office Papers FO 311/3451.
3. Smuts, 'Our policy at the Peace Conference'.
4. Smuts, Speech to American Editors, 14 November 1918, *SP*, Vol. 4, p 9.
5. Smuts, Speech to American Editors, 14 November 1918, *SP*, Vol. 4, pp 10–11.
6. Smuts, Speech to American Editors, 14 November 1918, *SP*, Vol. 4, p 11.
7. Smuts to Alice Clark, 1 April 1919, *SP*, Vol. 4, p 100.
8. Smuts, Speech to American Editors, p 11.
9. J C Smuts, *The League of Nations: A Practical Suggestion,* (Hodder and Stoughton, London: 1918) p 36.
10. Smuts, Speech to American Editors, 14 November 1918, *SP*, Vol. 4, p 14.
11. Smuts, Speech to American Editors, 14 November 1918, *SP*, Vol. 4, p 13.
12. Smuts, Speech to American Editors, 14 November 1918, *SP*, Vol. 4, p 12.
13. Smuts, Speech to American Editors, 14 November 1918, *SP*, Vol. 4, p 12.
14. Smuts, Speech to American Editors, 14 November 1918, *SP*, Vol. 4, p 13.
15. Smuts, Speech to American Editors, 14 November 1918, *SP*, Vol. 4, p 14.

16. E Goldstein, *Winning the Peace. British Diplomatic Strategy, Peace Planning, and the Paris Peace Conference 1916–1920*, (Oxford University Press, Oxford: 1991) p 218.

17. Smuts, *The League of Nations*, p 34.

18. Smuts, *The League of Nations*, p 36.

19. Smuts, *The League of Nations*, p 26–8.

20. Smuts, *The League of Nations*, pp 34, 40.

21. Smuts, *The League of Nations*, p 41.

22. *SP*, Vol. 4, p 32.

23. Smuts, *The League of Nations*, p 24.

24. Smuts, *The League of Nations*, p 46.

25. Smuts, *The League of Nations*, p 27.

26. Smuts, *The League of Nations*, p 47.

27. Smuts, *The League of Nations*, p 60.

28. Smuts to Lloyd George, 4 December 1918, House of Lords Record Office, Lloyd George Papers F/45/9/25.

29. *Smuts Sanguine*, p 509.

30. Smuts to Alice Clark, 21 January 1919, *SP*, Vol. 4, p 52.

31. Smuts to Isie Smuts, 15 January 1919, *SP*, Vol. 4, p 45.

32. Smuts to Isie Smuts, 14 November 1918, *SP*, Vol. 4, p 8.

33. Smuts to Margaret Gillett, 19 January 1919, *SP*, Vol. 4, pp 47–8.

34. Smuts to Alice Clark, 31 January 1919, *SP*, Vol. 4, p 58.

35. Smuts to Margaret Gillett, 18 January 1919, *SP*, Vol. 4, p 46.

36. Smuts to Alice Clark, 21 January 1919, *SP*, Vol. 4, p 51.

37. Wilson, Remarks, 28 February 1919, *PWW*, Vol. 55, p 321; Josephus Daniels, Diary, 25 February, *PWW*, Vol. 55, p 266.

38. *Smuts Sanguine*, p 507.

39. Smuts to Alice Clark, 16 February 1919, *SP*, Vol. 4, p 71.

40. *Cecil Diary*, 19 January 1919, British Library, Add Mss 51131.
41. Smuts to Margaret Gillett, 14 January 1919, *SP*, Vol. 4, p 42.
42. A Lentin, *Guilt at Versailles*, p 111.
43. Smuts to Alice Clark, 23 January 1919, *SP*, Vol. 4, p 54.
44. *Cecil Diary*, 31 January 1919.
45. Smuts to Margaret Gillett, 4 February 1919, *SP*, Vol. 4, p 60.
46. Smuts to Margaret Gillett, 8 February 1919, *SP*, Vol. 4, p 63.
47. *GS*, Vol 2, p 247.
48. Smuts, *The League of Nations*, p 28.
49. D Lloyd George, *Memoirs of the Peace Conference* (Yale University Press, New Haven: 1939) Vol. 1, pp 69, 70.
50. D Heater, *National Self-Determination. Woodrow Wilson and his Legacy* (St Martin's Press, London: 1994) p 91.
51. 'Imperial War Cabinet Committee on Territorial Desiderata', 18 April 1917, in Louis, *Great Britain and Germany's Lost Colonies*, p 83.
52. Smuts to Margaret Gillett, 20 January 1919, *SP*, Vol. 4, 50.
53. *Cecil Diary*, 25 January 1919.
54. Smuts to Margaret Gillett, 25 January 1919, *SP*, Vol. 4, p 55.
55. *PWW*, Vol. 54, pp 252–3.
56. Smuts to Margaret Gillett, 29 March 1919, *SP*, Vol. 4, p 92.
57. L F Fitzhardinge, *The Little Digger 1914–1952. William Morris Hughes. A Political Biography* (Angus and Robertson, Sydney: 1979) Vol. 2, p 398.

58. Wilson, Comment on Note by House, 29 January 1919, *PWW*, Vol. 54, p 347.
59. A Walworth, *Wilson and his Peacemakers. American Diplomacy at the Paris Peace Conference, 1919* (Norton, New York: 1986) p 79.
60. Smuts to Margaret Gillett, 29 January 1919, *SP*, Vol. 4, p 57.

4: The Fight for Revision (i): March–April 1919

1. Sir M Hankey, Telegram to Smuts, 10 March 1919, Cambridge University Library, Smuts Papers 685, vol. 21(microfilm).
2. Smuts to Margaret Gillett, 27 March 1919, *SP*, Vol. 4, p 87.
3. Smuts to Alice Clark, 28 March 1919, *SP*, Vol. 4, p 90.
4. Smuts to Lloyd George, 26 March 1919, *SP*, Vol. 4, p 83.
5. Lentin, *Guilt at Versailles,* p 19.
6. Smuts to Lloyd George, 26 March 1919, *SP*, Vol. 4, pp 84–7.
7. Smuts to Alice Clark, 28 March 1919, *SP*, Vol. 4, p 90.
8. Smuts to Margaret Gillett, 27 March 1919, *SP*, Vol. 4, p 89.
9. 27 March 1919, in P Mantoux, *Les Déliberations du Conseil des Quatre: Notes de l'officier interprète* (Centre National de la Recherche Scientifique, Paris: 1955) Vol. 1, p 46, hereafter Mantoux, *Déliberations.*
10. Mantoux, *Déliberations*, pp 46–7.
11. Smuts to Margaret Gillett, 31 March 1919, *SP*, Vol. 4, p 95.
12. Smuts to Margaret Gillett, 27 March 1919, *SP*, Vol. 4, p 89.

13. Smuts to Arthur Gillett, 23 January 1919, *SP*, Vol. 4, p 53.

14. 29 March 1919, in Mantoux, *Déliberations*, p 82.

15. R Lansing, Memorandum, 1 April 1919, *PWW*, Vol. 56, p 488.

16. *Foreign Relations of the United States. The Paris Peace Conference, 1919* (US Department of State, Washington DC: 1946) Vol. 5, p 16.

17. C E Callwell, *Field-Marshal Sir Henry Wilson. His Life and Diaries* (Cassell, London: 1927) Vol. 2, p 179.

18. Smuts to Lloyd George, 31 March 1919, *SP*, Vol. 4, p 99.

19. Smuts to Margaret Gillett, 27 March 1919, *SP*, Vol. 4, p 89.

20. H Nicolson, *Peacemaking*, p 294.

21. H Nicolson, *Peacemaking*, p 304.

22. Smuts, Report, in Lloyd George, *Memoirs of the Peace Conference*, Vol. 2, p 612.

23. *The Times*, 9 April 1919.

24. Smuts to Alice Clark, 9 April 1919, *SP*, Vol. 4, pp 118–19.

25. Smuts to Margaret Gillett, 9 April 1919, *SP*, Vol. 4, p 120.

26. Smuts to Alice Clark, 9 April 1919, *SP*, Vol. 4, p 118.

27. Frances Stevenson, Diary, 10 April 1919, in Frances Stevenson, *Lloyd George. A Diary*, A J P Taylor (ed) (Hutchinson, London: 1971) p 178.

28. Smuts to Margaret Gillett, 9 April 1919, *SP*, Vol. 4, p 120.

29. Smuts, Report, in M Lojko, 'Mission Impossible: General Smuts, Sir George Clerk and British Diplomacy in Central Europe in 1919', in Dokrill and Fisher, *Peace without Victory?*, p 122.

30. Smuts to Alice Clark, 23 April 1919, *SP*, Vol. 4, p 125.
31. Smuts to Lloyd George, 26 March 1919, *SP*, Vol. 4, p 86.
32. Lentin, 'Maynard Keynes and the "Bamboozlement" of Woodrow Wilson: What Really Happened at Paris? (Wilson, Lloyd George, Pensions and Pre-Armistice Agreement)', *Diplomacy and Statecraft,* Volume 15 (4), 2004, pp 736–7, hereafter Lentin, 'Maynard Keynes'.
33. Smuts to Margaret Gillett, 31 March 1919, *SP*, Vol. 4, p 95.
34. *Smuts Sanguine*, p 515.
35. Smuts, Memorandum, 31 March 1919, *SP*, Vol. 4, p 98.
36. Lentin, 'Maynard Keynes', p 730.
37. Lansing, Memorandum, 1 April 1919, *PWW*, Vol. 56, p 488.
38. Lentin, 'Maynard Keynes', p 726.
39. J M Keynes, *The Economic Consequences of the Peace,* (Labour Research Department, Westminster: 1920) p 48.
40. Lentin, 'Maynard Keynes', pp 729, 731, 737.
41. On the merits of Smuts's opinion on pensions see Lentin, 'Maynard Keynes', pp 740, 741–2.

5: The Fight for Revision (ii): May 1919

1. Smuts to Lloyd George, 11 April 1919, *SP*, Vol. 4, p 121.
2. Smuts to Alice Clark, 23 April 1919, *SP*, Vol. 4, p 125.
3. Smuts to Margaret Gillett, 2 May 1919, *SP*, Vol. 4, p 142.
4. Smuts to Alice Clark, 2 May 1919, *SP*, Vol. 4, p 141.
5. Smuts to Margaret Gillett, 1 May 1919, *SP*, Vol. 4, p 140.
6. Smuts to Alice Clark, 23 April 1919, *SP*, Vol. 4, p 125.
7. Smuts to Margaret Gillett, 4 May 1919, *SP*, Vol. 4, p 144.

8. Smuts to Margaret Gillett, 2 May 1919, *SP*, Vol. 4, p 142.

9. Smuts to Lloyd George, 5 May 1919, *SP*, Vol. 4, pp 148–9.

10. Lentin, *Guilt at Versailles*, p 84.

11. Smuts to Alice Clark, 7 May 1919, *SP*, Vol. 4, p 151.

12. Smuts to Alice Clark, 7 May 1919, *SP*, Vol. 4, p 151.

13. Smuts to Alice Clark, 7 May 1919, *SP*, Vol. 4, p 151–2.

14. Frances Stevenson Diary, 7 May 1919, in Lentin, *Guilt at Versailles*, p 87.

15. Smuts to Margaret Gillett, 7 May 1919, *SP*, Vol. 4, pp 152–3.

16. Smuts to Margaret Gillett, 14 May 1919, *SP*, Vol. 4, p 157.

17. Smuts to Lloyd George, 14 May 1919, *SP*, Vol. 4, pp 157–8.

18. Smuts to Alice Clark, 18 May 1919, *SP*, Vol. 4, p 166.

19. Smuts to Wilson, 16 May 1919, *PWW*, Vol. 59, p 198.

20. Smuts to Margaret Gillett, 18 May 1919, *SP*, Vol. 4, p 167.

21. Smuts, Private Memorandum, c. 18 May 1919, *SP*, Vol. 4, p 165.

22. Wilson to Smuts, 16 May 1919, *SP*, Vol. 4, pp 160–1.

23. Smuts to Margaret Gillett, 19 May 1919, *SP*, Vol. 4, p 171.

24. Smuts to Alice Clark, 18 May 1919, *SP*, Vol. 4, p 166.

25. Smuts to Margaret Gillett, 18 May 1919, *SP*, Vol. 4, p 167.

26. Smuts to Henry Gillett, 20 May 1919, Cambridge University Library, Smuts Papers Add.7917.

27. *Cecil Diary*, 20 May 1919.

28. Smuts to Margaret Gillett, 16 May 1919, *SP*, Vol. 4, p 162.

29. Smuts to Isie Smuts, 20 May 1919, *SP*, Vol. 4, p 176.

30. Smuts to Margaret Gillett, 19 May 1919, *SP*, Vol. 4, p 171. Horace described his poetic achievement as 'a monument more durable than brass'. Matthew 7.26 refers to 'a foolish man, which built his house upon the sand'.

31. Smuts to Margaret Gillett, 19 May 1919, *SP*, Vol. 4, pp 171–2.

32. Headlam-Morley to Smuts, 19 May 1919, *SP*, p 169.

33. Smuts to Isie Smuts, 20 May 1919, *SP*, Vol. 4, p 176–7.

34. Smuts to Isie Smuts, 20 May 1919, *SP*, Vol. 4, p 179.

35. Smuts to Henry Gillett, 20 May 1919, Cambridge University Library, Smuts Papers, Add 7917.

36. Smuts to Margaret Gillett, 22 May 1919, *SP*, Vol. 4, p 182.

37. Smuts to Alice Clark, 23 May 1919, *SP*, Vol. 4, p 190.

38. Smuts, Memorandum, 22 May 1919, *SP*, Vol. 4, pp 188–9.

39. Smuts, Memorandum, *SP*, Vol. 4, p 189.

40. Smuts to Alice Clark, 23 May 1919, *SP*, Vol. 4, p 190.

41. *Cecil Diary*, 20 May 1919.

42. *Cecil Diary*, 24 May 1919.

43. Lentin, *Guilt at Versailles,* p 55.

44. Smuts to Margaret Gillett, 25 May 1919, *SP*, Vol. 4, p 195.

45. Smuts to Margaret Gillett, 28 May 1919, *SP*, Vol. 4, p 203.

46. Smuts to Margaret Gillett, 28 May 1919, *SP*, Vol. 4, p 202.

47. Smuts to Lloyd George, 26 May 1919, *SP*, Vol. 4, p 197.

48. Smuts to Isie Smuts, 10 June 1919, *SP*, Vol. 4, p 226.
49. Smuts to Lloyd George, 26 May 1919, *SP*, Vol. 4, p 197.
50. Smuts to Lloyd George, 27 May 1919, *SP*, Vol. 4, p 199.
51. *GS*, Vol. 2, p 207.
52. Smuts to Margaret Gillett, 28 May 1919, *SP*, Vol. 4, p 203.

6: 'Wilson Peace' or 'Scrap of Paper'? 29 May–2 June 1919

1. Smuts to Alice Clark, 16 May 1919, *SP*, Vol. 4, p 161.
2. Smuts to Isie Smuts, 27 May 1919, *SP*, Vol. 4, pp 200, 201.
3. H Harmer, *Friedrich Ebert* (Haus Publishing, London: 2008) pp 72–3.
4. *BDFA*, p 98.
5. Smuts to Alice Clark, 30 May 1919, *SP*, Vol. 4, p 207.
6. Margaret Gillett to Smuts, 30 May 1919, *SP*, Vol. 4, p 206.
7. Smuts to Wilson, 30 May 1919, *SP*, Vol. 4, p 209.
8. Wilson to Smuts, 31 May 1919, *SP*, Vol. 4, p 210.
9. Smuts to Margaret Gillett, 30 May 1919, *SP*, Vol. 4, p 204.
10. Smuts to Margaret Gillett, 28 May 1919, *SP*, Vol. 4, p 203.
11. Smuts to Margaret Gillett, 30 May 1919, *SP*, Vol. 4, p 205.
12. *BDFA*, p 92.
13. *BDFA*, p 93.
14. Herbert Fisher, Diary, 31 May 1919, Bodleian Library, Oxford, Fisher Papers 8A.
15. Montagu, Diary, 4 June 1919, in S D Waley, *Edwin Montagu: A Memoir and an Account of His Visits to India* (Asia Publishing House, London: 1964) p 211.

16. *Cecil Diary*, 31 May 1919.

17. Herbert Fisher, Diary, 31 May 1919, in Lentin, *Lloyd George and the Lost Peace*, p 71.

18. Montagu, Note, 4 June 1919, in Lentin, *Guilt at Versailles*, p 94.

19. Smuts to Margaret Gillett, 1 June 1919, *SP*, Vol. 4, p 211.

20. Montagu, Note, 4 June 1919, in Waley, *Edwin Montagu*, p 211.

21. *BDFA*, p 98.

22. *BDFA*, pp 98–9.

23. Bernard Baruch, Diary, 2 June 1919, in P J Yearwood, *Guarantee of Peace. The League of Nations in British Policy 1914–1925* (Oxford University Press, Oxford: 2009) p 126.

24. *BDFA*, pp 98, 99, 103, 99.

25. *BDFA*, p 102.

26. *BDFA*, p 101.

27. *BDFA*, p 102.

28. *BDFA*, p 103.

29. *BDFA*, p 106.

30. Montagu, Note, 4 June 1919, in Lentin, *Guilt at Versailles*, pp 94–5.

31. *BDFA*, p 104.

32. *BDFA*, p 92.

33. Lentin, *Guilt at Versailles*, pp 124–5.

34. *BDFA*, p 107.

35. *BDFA*, p 105.

36. *BDFA*, p 101.

37. Nicolson, Diary, 4 April 1919, in H Nicolson, *Peacemaking 1919*, p 301.

38. *BDFA*, p 99.

39. *BDFA*, p 109.
40. *BDFA*, p 93.
41. Smuts to Margaret Gillett, 1 June 1919, *SP*, Vol. 4, p 211.
42. Milner, Diary, 1 June 1919, in Lentin, *Lloyd George and the Lost Peace*, p 73.
43. Smuts to Margaret Gillett, 18 May 1919, *SP*, Vol. 4, p 166.
44. Smuts to Margaret Gillett, 19 May 1919, *SP*, Vol. 4, p 171.
45. Smuts, February 1929, in *Holistic Smuts*, p 68.
46. Fisher, Diary, 1 June 1919, Bodleian Library, Fisher Papers, *BDFA*, p 114.
47. *Holistic Smuts*, p 67.
48. Fisher, Diary, 1 June 1919, Bodleian Library Fisher Papers.
49. Smuts to Margaret Gillett, 2 June 1919, *SP*, Vol. 4, pp 212–13.
50. Waley, *Edwin Montagu*, p 212.
51. Lentin, *Guilt at Versailles*, p 77.
52. 1 June 1919, *BDFA*, p 113.
53. 1 June 1919, *BDFA*, p 115.

7: 'The Last Battle of the War': June 1919

1. Smuts to Margaret Gillett, 2 June 1919, *SP*, Vol. 4, p 212.
2. *SP*, Vol. 4, p 213.
3. Smuts to Lloyd George, 2 June 1919, *SP*, Vol. 4, p 216.
4. Thomas Jones, Diary, 2 July 1919, in Middlemas (ed), *Whitehall Diary*, Vol. 1, p 87.
5. Lloyd George to Smuts, 3 June 1919, *SP*, Vol. 4, p 217.

6. Lloyd George to Smuts, 3 June 1919, *SP*, Vol. 4, pp 217–18.
7. Smuts to Margaret Gillett, 3 June 1919, *SP*, Vol. 4, p 219.
8. Smuts to Lloyd George, 4 June 1919, *SP*, Vol. 4, p 219.
9. Smuts to Lloyd George, 22 May 1919, *SP*, Vol. 4, p 183.
10. Smuts to Lloyd George, 4 June 1919, *SP*, Vol. 4, p 220.
11. Smuts to Lloyd George, 4 June 1919, *SP*, Vol. 4, p 221.
12. Smuts to Alice Clark, 16 June 1919, *SP*, Vol. 4, p 231.
13. Smuts to Isie Smuts, 20 May 1919, *SP*, Vol. 4, p 177.
14. Smuts to Isie Smuts, 10 June 1919, *SP*, Vol. 4, p 225.
15. *JCS*, p 193.
16. *Smuts Sanguine,* p 438.
17. Smuts to Margaret Gillett, 16 June 1919, *SP*, Vol. 4, p 233.
18. Smuts to Margaret Gillett, 19 May 1919, *SP*, Vol. 4, p 171.
19. Alice Clark to Smuts, 25 May 1919, *SP*, Vol. 4, p 196.
20. *GS*, Vol. 2, p 288.
21. *Holistic Smuts,* p 186.
22. Smuts to Margaret Gillett, 20 April 1919, *SP*, Vol. 4, p 123.
23. Smuts to Margaret Gillett, 16 June 1919, *SP*, Vol. 4, p 233.
24. Smuts to Lady Mary Murray, 2 June 1919, *SP*, Vol. 4, p 213.
25. Smuts to Margaret Gillett, 3 June 1919, *SP*, Vol. 4, p 219.
26. Smuts to Keynes, 10 June 1919, *SP*, Vol. 4, p 223.
27. Smuts to Keynes, 10 June 1919, *SP*, Vol. 4, p 223.
28. Smuts to Isie Smuts, 10 June 1919, *SP*, Vol. 4, p 225.

29. Smuts to Margaret Gillett, 16 June 1919, *SP*, Vol. 4, p 233.
30. Smuts to Botha, 21 June 1919, *SP*, Vol. 4, p 240.
31. Smuts to Margaret Gillett, 23 June 1919, *SP*, Vol. 4, p 244.
32. *GS,* Vol. 2, p 189.
33. A Toynbee, *Acquaintances* (Oxford University Press, Oxford: 1967) p 177.
34. Smuts to Margaret Gillett, 23 June 1919, *SP*, Vol. 4, p 245.
35. Smuts to Margaret Gillett, 24 June 1919, *SP*, Vol. 4, p 247.
36. Smuts to Margaret Gillett, 28 June 1919, *SP*, Vol. 4, p 255.
37. Smuts, Speech at Botha's Funeral, 30 August 1919, *SP*, Vol. 4, p 289.
38. Smuts, February 1929, in *Holistic Smuts,* p 68.
39. Smuts to Margaret Gillett, 28 June 1919, *SP*, Vol. 4, p 255.
40. Smuts to Margaret Gillett, 28 June 1919, *SP*, Vol. 4, p 255.
41. Smuts to Lord Parmoor, 17 April 1919, *SP*, Vol. 4, p 122.
42. Smuts, Statement, 28 June 1919, *SP*, Vol. 4, pp 256–7.

8: 'A Carthaginian Peace'? 1919–1939

1. Scott, Diary, 4 July 1919, in *Scott*, p 375.
2. Smuts to Alice Clark, 10 January 1920, in *Smuts Force*, p 10.
3. Smuts to Alice Clark, 16 June 1919, *SP*, Vol. 4, p 232.
4. *GS,* Vol. 1, pp 208–9.
5. Smuts to Margaret Gillett, 24 June 1919, *SP*, Vol. 4, p 248.

6. Smuts to Margaret Gillett, 14 May 1919, Cambridge University Library, Smuts Papers Add 7917.

7. H Nicolson, *Peacemaking 1919*, p 161.

8. Lentin, *Guilt at Versailles,* p 11.

9. 'Allied Reply to the German Counterproposals', 16 June 1919, in Alma Luckau, *The German Delegation at the Paris Peace Conference* (Columbia University Press, New York: 1940) pp 419–20.

10. *BDFA*, p 98.

11. *BDFA*, p 99.

12. Smuts to Margaret Gillett, 19 May 1919, *SP*, Vol. 4, p 171.

13. Smuts, Statement, 28 June 1919, *SP*, Vol. 4, p 257.

14. Smuts to Isie Smuts, 10 June 1919, *SP*, Vol. 4, p 225.

15. *BDFA*, p 108.

16. Smuts to Isie Smuts, 1 June 1902, *Smuts Sanguine,* p 164.

17. Smuts, quoted in *Religious Smuts,* p 96.

18. Smuts, Farewell Statement, 18 July 1919, *SP*, Vol. 4, p 271.

19. Smuts, Farewell Statement, 18 July 1919, *SP*, Vol. 4, p 270.

20. H Nicolson, in N Nicolson (ed), *Diaries and Letters 1939–1945* (Collins, London: 1967) p 334.

21. *BDFA,* pp 98, 99.

22. 'Our Policy at the Peace Conference', National Archives, Foreign Office Papers FO 311/3451

23. Smuts, Farewell Statement, 18 July 1919, *SP*, Vol. 4, p 269.

24. 'Our policy at the Peace Conference; "Meeting of Eastern Committee" ', 2 December 1918, in Goldstein, *Winning the Peace*, p 157.

25. *GS,* Vol 2, p 266.

26. *GS*, Vol 2, p 270.
27. *GS*, Vol 2, p 174.
28. Smuts to Alice Clark, 10 July 1919, *SP*, Vol. 4, p 263.
29. C P Scott, Diary, 5 July 1919, in *Scott*, p 375.
30. *The New York Times*, 3 March 1921.
31. H Nicolson, *Peacemaking 1919*, pp 320–321.
32. C P Scott, Diary, 5 July 1919, in *Scott*, p 375.
33. C P Scott, Diary, 5 July 1919, in *Scott*, p 375.
34. Keynes to Smuts, 8 June 1919, *SP*, Vol. 4, p 222.
35. Smuts to Keynes, 10 June 1919, *SP*, Vol. 4, p 10.
36. Smuts to Keynes, 17 July 1919, *SP*, Vol. 4, p 266; *GS*, Vol. 2, pp 174, 257.
37. *GS*, Vol. 2, p 174.
38. *GS*, Vol. 2, p 257.
39. *GS*, Vol. 2, p 290.
40. Imperial Conference, 1921, Smuts to Margaret Gillett, 24 March 1922, in *Smuts Force*, p 84.
41. Smuts to Margaret Gillett, 24 March 1922, in *Smuts Force*, p 84.
42. Smuts to Lloyd George, June 1921, in *Smuts Force*, p 53.
43. *Scott*, p 391.
44. Smuts to Arthur and Margaret Gillett, 26 August 1921, in *The Fields of Force*, p 60.
45. Smuts to Lloyd George, 5 July 1922, Lloyd George Papers LG/F/45/9/58.
46. Smuts to Bonar Law, 20 November 1922, in *Smuts Force*, p 130.
47. Smuts to Isie Smuts, 18 October 1923, in *Smuts Force*, p 135.
48. Smuts, Speech to South African Luncheon Club, London, 23 October 1923, in *Smuts Force*, p 135.

49. Smuts, Speech to South African Luncheon Club, in *Smuts Force*, p 135.

50. Smuts to Adolf Meyer-Abich, July 1948, *JCS*, p 291.

51. Smuts, Speech, 1934, in Friedlander, p 88.

52. Blankenberg, *Thoughts*, p 28.

53. J H Hofmeyr was a cousin of the J Hofmeyr mentioned earlier.

54. Millin, *The Measure of My Days,* p 266.

55. Smuts, Speech, 23 September 1919, in *GS*, Vol. 2, p 299.

56. Smuts, Speech, 16 January 1930, *JCS*, p 298.

57. *JCS*, p 193.

58. Smuts to Arthur Gillett, 1 July 1934, in *Smuts Force*, p 269.

59. Smuts to Margaret Gillett, 18 March 1934, in *Smuts Force*, p 269.

60. Smuts, Speech to Royal Institute of International Affairs, 13 November 1934, *International Affairs,* Vol. 14, No. 1 (Jan–Feb 1935) p 10.

61. Churchill, Speech, 15 November 1934, Lloyd George Papers LG/G/4/5/7.

62. Smuts, Speech to Royal Institute of International Affairs, p 12.

63. Smuts to Lord Lothian, 20 February 1935, in *Smuts Force*, p 271.

64. Smuts to Margaret Gillett, 27 July 1936, in *Smuts Force,* p 280.

65. Smuts to L Amery, 28 March 1938, in M G Fry, 'Agents and Structures: The Dominions and the Czechoslovak Crisis, September 1938', I Lukes and E Goldstein (ed), *The Munich Crisis, 1938. Prelude to World War II,* (Frank Cass, London: 1999) p 301.

66. Smuts to Margaret Gillett, 10 October 1938, quoted by Fry, p 331.
67. Smuts to Sir Patrick Duncan, 7 November 1938, in Fry, p 333.
68. Smuts to Margaret Gillett, 17 March 1939, in *Smuts Force*, p 310.
69. Speech, 27 March 1939, in *Smuts Force*, p 316.
70. *Smuts Force*, p 314.
71. T R H Davenport, *South Africa. A Modern History* (MacMillan, London:1978) p 232.

9: Smuts and the Second World War: 1939–45

1. T J Haarhoff, p viii.
2. P Van der Byl, *Top Hat to Velskoen* (Timmins, Cape Town: 1973) p 163.
3. *JCS*, p 419.
4. *Holistic Smuts,* p 94.
5. Smuts to Margaret Gillett, 7 May 1943, in *Smuts Force*, p 389.
6. Smuts to Margaret Gillett, 31 January 1942, in *Smuts Force*, p 392.
7. Lady Moore, wife of the Governor of Kenya, July 1941, in *Romantic Smuts,* p 126.
8. Keppel-Jones, p 173.
9. Sir De Villers Graaff, 'General Smuts as I knew him', in Friedlander, *Thoughts*, p 99.
10. Lord Moran, *Winston Churchill. The Struggle for Survival 1940–65* (Constable, London: 1966) p 774.
11. *JCS*, p 438.
12. Mary Soames, *Clementine Churchill* (Cassell, London: 1979) p 405.

13. Lord Moran's Diary, 30 November 1946, in Moran, *Winston Churchill*, p 317.
14. Smuts, 'Address at Installation as Chancellor of the University of Cape Town', March 1937, in Blankenberg, p 65.
15. *JCS*, p 201.
16. *JCS*, p 436.
17. Sir A Lascelles, Diary, 28 January 1943, in D Hart-Davis (ed), *King's Counsellor. Abdication and War: The Diaries of Sir Alan Lascelles,* (Weidenfeld and Nicolson, London: 2006) p 94.
18. R. Jenkins, *Churchill* (Pan Books, London: 2002) p 789.
19. Lady Harlech, 28 December 1942, in Hart-Davis, *King's Counsellor*, p 94.
20. Lascelles, Diary, 21 October 1942, in Hart-Davis, *King's Counsellor*, p 64.
21. Smuts, Speech to both Houses of Parliament, *Journal of the Royal African Society,* vol.42, No. 167, *King's Counsellor*, p 60.
22. Lascelles, Diary, 21 October 1942, in Hart-Davis, p 172.
23. *JCS*, p 442.
24. Smuts to Margaret Gillett, 14 February 1944, in *Smuts Force*, p 414.
25. Smuts to Margaret Gillett, 4 March 1945, in *Smuts Force*, p 419.
26. *JCS*, p 475.

10: 'Superhuman Courage': Smuts 1945–50

1. Smuts to Margaret Gillett, 11 March 1945, in *Smuts Force*, p 444.
2. *JCS*, p 472.
3. *JCS*, p 470.

4. Smuts was referring to Churchill, Roosevelt and Stalin and to St Paul in 1 *Corinthians* 13: 'And now abideth faith, hope and charity, these three; but the greatest of these is charity.' Smuts to Margaret Gillett, 28 December 1945, in *Smuts Force*, p 438.

5. *Salute to a Great South African. Jan Christian Smuts* (Cape Times Ltd, Cape Town: 1950) p 16; *Religious Smuts*, p 107.

6. H Nicolson, Diary, 4 June 1946, in N Nicolson (ed), *Diaries and Letters 1945–62* (Collins, London: 1969) p 63.

7. H Nicolson, Diary, 4 June 1946, in N Nicolson (ed), *Diaries and Letters 1945–62*, p 64.

8. *Smuts Force*, p 509.

9. Smuts to Margaret Gillett, 7 June 1942, in *Religious Smuts*, p 48.

10. *Romantic Smuts*, p 51.

11. *GS*, Vol. 2, pp 94–5.

12. Blankenberg, *Thoughts*, p 125.

13. Lascelles, Diary, 14 November 1942, in Hart-Davis, *King's Counsellor*, p 76.

14. Millin, *The Measure of My Days*, p 212.

15. *People*, p 164.

16. Millin, *The Measure of My Days*, p 212,

17. Smuts to Margaret Gillett, 4 March 1945, *SP*, Vol. 6, p 527.

18. Freda Troup, *South Africa. An Historical Introduction* (Eyre Methuen, London: 1972) p 249.

19. Smuts, 1920, in Heater, *National Self-Determination*, p 201.

20. Smuts to Thomas Lamont, 31 March 1947, in *Holistic Smuts*, p 182.

21. Smuts to Margaret Gillett, 14 January 1947, in *Holistic Smuts,* p 163.
22. Smuts to Margaret Gillett, 14 January 1947, in *Holistic Smuts,* p 194.
23. *Holistic Smuts,* p 89.
24. N Mandela, *Long Walk to Freedom. The Autobiography of Nelson Mandela* (Little Brown and Co, New York: 1994) pp 57–8.
25. Smuts to J Merriman, *SP,* Vol. 2, p 244.
26. L Egeland, 'Counsellor of Kings', in Friedlander, *Jan Smuts Remembered,* p 33.
27. Millin, *The Measure of My Days,* p 274.
28. *Holistic Smuts,* p 54.
29. Egeland, 'Counsellor of Kings', p 31.
30. *GS,* Vol 2, p 36.
31. *GS,* Vol 2, p 334.
32. *Smuts Force,* p 495.
33. *Holistic Smuts,* p 95.
34. Millin, *The Measure of My Days,* p 277.
35. Daphne Moore, 'Family Friendship', in Friedlander, *Jan Smuts Remembered*, p 62.
36. *Religious Smuts,* p 89.
37. *JCS,* p 273.

Conclusion

1. Smuts to Margaret Gillett, 21 June 1919, *SP*, Vol. 4, p 240.
2. Lentin, *Guilt at Versailles,* p 70.
3. Hyam, 'South Africa, Cambridge and Commonwealth History', p 401.

Chronology

YEAR	AGE	THE LIFE AND THE LAND
1870		24 May: Jan Christian Smuts born at Bovenplaats, Cape Province.
		Gold discovered at Kimberley in Griqualand West; three years earlier, 1867, it had been discovered on Orange River.
1877	7	Britain annexes Griqualand West.
1880–1	10	First Boer War. British defeated at Majuba Hill.
1882	12	Smuts goes to Riebeeck village school.
1883	13	Gold discovered on Witwatersrand.
		Uitlanders flood into Transvaal.
1886	16	Smuts enters Victoria College, Stellenbosch.
1891	21	Smuts graduates from Victoria College. Goes to England to read Law at Cambridge.
1894	24	Smuts graduates with a Cambridge double first in Law.
1895	25	Smuts returns to South Africa, is admitted to Cape Bar. The Jameson Raid.

YEAR	HISTORY	CULTURE
1870	Red River Rebellion in Canada ends. Franco-Prussian War: Napoleon III defeated at Sedan, Third Republic proclaimed, Paris besieged. Western Australia granted representative government.	Charles Dickens dies. Jules Verne, *Twenty Thousand Leagues Under the Sea*. Leo Delibes, *Coppélia*. Richard Wagner, *Die Walküre*.
1877	Russo-Turkish War begins.	Henry James, *The American*.
1880–1	France annexes Tahiti.	Fyodor Dostoevsky, *The Brothers Karamazov*.
1882	Triple Alliance between Italy, Germany and Austria-Hungary.	Peter Tchaikovsky, *1812 Overture*.
1883	British decide to evacuate the Sudan.	Friedrich Nietzsche, *Thus Spake Zarathustra*.
1886	First Indian National Congress meets.	Auguste Rodin, *The Kiss*.
1891	Triple Alliance (Austria-Hungary, Germany, Italy) renewed for 12 years. Franco-Russian entente.	Henri de Toulouse-Lautrec produces first music-hall posters.
1894	Dreyfus Case begins in France.	Anthony Hope, *The Prisoner of Zenda*.
1895	Sino-Japanese War ends. Guglielmo Marconi invents radio telegraphy.	H G Wells, *The Time Machine*. W B Yeats, *Poems*.

YEAR	AGE	THE LIFE AND THE LAND
1896	26	Smuts renounces British citizenship, moves to Transvaal, sets up as lawyer in Johannesburg, then in Pretoria.
1897	27	Smuts marries Sybella Margaretha Krige ('Isie').
1898	28	Kruger appoints Smuts as State Attorney of the Transvaal republic.
1899	29	British pressurise Transvaal over *Uitlanders*. Smuts accompanies Kruger in talks with Governor-General Milner at Bloemfontein. Writes *A Century of Wrong*.
		Drafts ultimatum calling for withdrawal of British troops from South Africa.
		Second Boer War (to 1902).
1900	30	June: fall of Pretoria. Kruger flees abroad. Smuts escapes from Pretoria with state funds.
1901	31	Smuts, now a general, leads commando unit into Cape Colony.
1902	32	Smuts participates in peace negotiations at Vereeniging.
		31 May: Peace of Vereeniging signed.
		Transvaal and Orange Free State become British Crown Colonies under Milner's governorship.
		Smuts practises successfully as lawyer. Refuses to join Transvaal legislative council.

YEAR	HISTORY	CULTURE
1896	Abyssinians defeat Italian army at Adowa. General Kitchener begins reconquest of the Sudan.	Anton Chekhov, *The Seagull*. Richard Strauss, *Also Sprach Zarathustra*.
1897	Britain's Queen Victoria celebrates Diamond Jubilee.	Edmond Rostand, *Cyrano de Bergerac*.
1898	Kitchener defeats Mahdists at Omdurman. Germany's Otto von Bismarck dies.	Henry James, *The Turn of the Screw*. Oscar Wilde, *The Ballad of Reading Gaol*.
1899	Anglo-Egyptian Sudan Convention. First Peace Conference at the Hague. Alfred Dreyfus pardoned by presidential decree. Germany secures Baghdad railway contract.	Rudyard Kipling, *Stalky and Co*. Arthur Pinero, *Trelawny of the Wells*. Edward Elgar, *Enigma Variations*.
1900	King Umberto I of Italy assassinated. Boxer Rising in China.	Giacomo Puccini, *Tosca*. John Singer Sargent, *The Sitwell Family*.
1901	Britain's Queen Victoria dies: Edward VII becomes King.	Rudyard Kipling, *Kim*.
1902	Anglo-Japanese Treaty recognises independence of China and Korea. First meeting of Committee of Imperial Defence. Triple Alliance between Austria, Germany and Italy renewed for another six years. USA acquires perpetual control over Panama Canal.	Arthur Conan Doyle, *The Hound of the Baskervilles*. Maxim Gorki, *Lower Depths*. Anton Chekhov, *Three Sisters*. Claude Monet, *Waterloo Bridge*. Edward Elgar, *Pomp and Circumstance March No 1*.

YEAR	AGE	THE LIFE AND THE LAND
1904	34	Botha and Smuts found Het Volk party.
1905	35	Smuts goes to England to plead cause of Transvaal to Liberal leaders. Interview with Campbell-Bannerman who agrees to grant self-government to Transvaal and Orange Free State.
1907	37	Het Volk wins election in Transvaal. Botha becomes Prime Minister. Smuts becomes Colonial Secretary and Minister of Education. Gift of Cullinan diamond to Edward VII. Smuts becomes a KC.
1908	38	Smuts calls National Convention to consider constitution for a United South Africa. Buys farm at Doornkloof near Pretoria.
1910	40	Union of South Africa established as British Dominion. General election. Smuts becomes Minister of Defence, Minister of Interior and Minister of Mines.
1911	41	Smuts deputises for Botha during his absence at Imperial Conference.
1912	42	Smuts establishes Union Defence Force. Hertzog leaves Government to lead Afrikaner National Party in opposition.

YEAR	HISTORY	CULTURE
1904	Entente Cordiale settles British-French colonial differences.	J M Barrie, *Peter Pan*.
1905	Anglo-Japanese alliance renewed for ten years. 'Bloody Sunday': police break-up Russian demonstration, by Tsar Nicholas II issues the 'October Manifesto'.	E M Forster, *Where Angels Fear to Tread*. Edith Wharton, *House of Mirth*. Richard Strauss, *Salome*. Claude Debussy, *La Mer*.
1907	New Zealand granted Dominion status. Grigori Rasputin gains influence at the court of Tsar Nicholas II. Peace Conference held in The Hague.	Joseph Conrad, *The Secret Agent*. Maxim Gorky, *Mother*. R M Rilke, *Neue Gedichte*. First Cubist exhibition in Paris.
1908	*The Daily Telegraph* publishes German Kaiser Wilhelm II's hostile remarks towards England.	Kenneth Grahame, *The Wind in the Willows*. Edward Elgar, *Symphony No. 1 in A-Flat*.
1910	Britain's King Edward VII dies; succeeded by George V. Liberals win British General Election.	H G Wells, *The History of Mr Polly*. Giacomo Puccini, *La Fanciulla del West*.
1911	German gunboat *Panther* arrives in Agadir: triggers international crisis.	Max Beerbohm, *Zuleika Dobson*. D H Lawrence, *The White Peacock*.
1912	*Titanic* sinks: 1,513 die. First Balkan War begins.	C G Jung, *The Theory of Psychoanalysis*. Maurice Ravel, *Daphne et Chloe*.

YEAR	AGE	THE LIFE AND THE LAND
1913	43	Miners' strike on the Rand. Rioting at Johannesburg; Smuts and Botha concede miners' demands.
		Natives Land Act restricts blacks to 7 per cent of land.
1914	44	Jan: Smuts suppresses general strike and deports strike leaders.
		Aug: Botha and Smuts support, Hertzog opposes, Britain's declaration of war, which brings in South Africa.
		Botha and Smuts suppress a Boer rebellion against the Union.
1915	45	Botha and Smuts subdue German South-West Africa.
		Smuts is shot at during election campaign.
1916	46	Smuts, now Lieutenant General in British Army, leads conquest of German East Africa.

YEAR	HISTORY	CULTURE
1913	London Ambassadors Conference ends First Balkan War: establishes independent Albania. King George I of Greece assassinated: succeeded by Constantine I. Second Balkan War begins and ends.	Thomas Mann, *Death in Venice.* Marcel Proust, *Du côté de chez Swann.* Igor Stravinsky, *Le Sacre du Printemps.*
1914	Archduke Franz Ferdinand of Austria-Hungary and wife assassinated in Sarajevo. First World War begins: Battles of Mons, the Marne and First Ypres; trench warfare on Western Front; Russians defeated in Battles of Tannenberg and Masurian Lakes.	James Joyce, *Dubliners.* Theodore Dreiser, *The Titan.* Gustav Holst, *The Planets.* Matisse, *The Red Studio.* Georges Braque, *Music.* Film: Charlie Chaplin in *Making a Living.*
1915	First World War: Battles of Neuve Chapelle and Loos, Gallipoli campaign.	Joseph Conrad, *Victory.* Film: *The Birth of a Nation.*
1916	First World War: Battles of Verdun, the Somme and Jutland. US President Woodrow Wilson issues Peace Note to belligerents in European war. David Lloyd George becomes British Prime Minister.	James Joyce, *Portrait of an Artist as a Young Man.* Film: *Intolerance.*

YEAR	AGE	THE LIFE AND THE LAND
1917	47	Mar: Smuts in England for Imperial War Conference.
		Apr: Smuts reports on Western Front.
		May: Smuts supports proposed League of Nations. Advocates British Commonwealth of Nations. Refuses Palestine command.
		Refuses to chair Irish Convention.
		Jun: Smuts joins War Cabinet. Reports critically on British strategy but approves campaign in Flanders.
		Jul: Smuts chairs War Priorities Committee. Recommends measures to counter air-raids and establishment of Royal Air Force.
		Oct: Smuts settles Welsh miners' strike.
		Nov: Smuts accompanies Lloyd George to Rapallo after Italy's defeat at Caporetto.
		Dec: Smuts secretly meets Count Mensdorff in Geneva to discuss a separate peace for Austria-Hungary.
1918	48	Jan: Smuts writes draft for Lloyd George's speech on war aims. Visits Western Front and predicts points where Ludendorff offensive will fall.
		Feb: Smuts in Middle East to plan completion of Palestine campaign.
		May: Smuts opposes Lloyd George's 'knock-out blow' to end war.
		Oct: Smuts favours early ceasefire with Germany.
		Nov: Smuts gives address on League of Nations.
		Dec: Smuts resigns from War Cabinet.

YEAR	HISTORY	CULTURE
1917	First World War: Battle of Passchendaele (Third Ypres); British and Commonwealth forces take Jerusalem; USA declares war on Germany; China declares war on Germany and Russia. February Revolution in Russia. Balfour Declaration favouring establishment of national home for Jewish People in Palestine. German and Russian delegates sign armistice at Brest-Litovsk.	P G Wodehouse, *The Man With Two Left Feet.* T S Eliot, *Prufrock and Other Observations.* Leon Feuchtwanger, *Jud Suess.* Piet Mondrian launches *De Stijl* magazine in Holland. Pablo Picasso designs 'surrealist' costumes, set for Erik Satie's *Parade.* Hans Pfitzner, *Palestrina.* Sergei Prokofiev, *Classical Symphony.* Film: *Easy Street.*
1918	First World War: Peace Treaty of Brest-Litovsk signed between Russia and Central Powers; German Spring offensives on Western Front fail; Romania signs Peace of Bucharest with Germany and Austria-Hungary; Allied offensives on Western Front have German army in full retreat; Armistice signed between Allies and Germany; German Fleet surrenders. Ex-Tsar Nicholas II and family executed. Kaiser Wilhelm II of Germany abdicates.	Alexander Blok, *The Twelve.* Gerard Manley Hopkins, *Poems.* Luigi Pirandello, *Six Characters in Search of an Author.* Bela Bartok, *Bluebeard's Castle.* Giacomo Puccini, *Il Trittico.* Gustav Cassel, *Theory of Social Economy.* Oskar Kokoshka, *Friends* and *Saxonian Landscape.* Edvard Munch, *Bathing Man.*

YEAR	AGE	THE LIFE AND THE LAND
1919	49	Jan: Botha and Smuts at Paris Peace Conference. Smuts on committee to draft League of Nations Covenant. Puts case for South African Mandate over South-West Africa and drafts formula for
		Mandates.
		Apr: Smuts on mission to Bela Kun in Budapest via Vienna. Proposes international loan to Europe as member of Supreme Economic Council.
		May: Smuts declines to serve on Austrian Commission on Reparations.
		Smuts denounces Treaty at meeting of British Empire delegation.
		Jun: Smuts denounces Treaty at expanded meeting of British Empire Delegation. Smuts signs the Treaty but issues statement.
		Jul: Smuts returns to South Africa, after issuing second statement on the Treaty.
		Aug: On Botha's death, Smuts becomes Prime Minister of South Africa, and Minister of Defence and Native Affairs.
1920	50	Hertzog's National Party gains in general election. Smuts' South African Party merges with Unionist Party.
1921	51	Smuts wins general election. Attends Imperial Conference. Advises on Irish settlement; meets De Valera.
1922	52	Smuts crushes violent strike on the Rand.

YEAR	HISTORY	CULTURE
1919	Communist Revolt in Berlin. Benito Mussolini founds Fascist movement in Italy. Britain and France authorise resumption of commercial relations with Germany. British-Persian agreement at Tehran to preserve integrity of Persia. Irish War of Independence begins. US Senate vetoes ratification of Versailles Treaty leaving US outside League of Nations.	Bauhaus movement founded by Walter Gropius. Wassily Kandinsky, *Dreamy Improvisation*. Paul Klee, *Dream Birds*. Thomas Hardy, *Collected Poems*. Herman Hesse, *Demian*. George Bernard Shaw, *Heartbreak House*. Eugene D'Albert, *Revolutionshochzeit*. Edward Elgar, *Concerto in E Minor for Cello*. Manuel de Falla, *The Three-Cornered Hat*. Film: *The Cabinet of Dr Caligari*.
1920	League of Nations comes into existence. Bolsheviks win Russian Civil War.	F Scott Fitzgerald, *This Side of Paradise*. Franz Kafka, *The Country Doctor*.
1921	Irish Free State established. Washington Naval Treaty signed.	D H Lawrence, *Women in Love*.
1922	Chanak crisis. League of Nations Council approves British Mandate in Palestine.	British Broadcasting Company (later Corporation) (BBC) founded: first radio broadcasts.

YEAR	AGE	THE LIFE AND THE LAND
1923	53	Smuts attends Imperial Conference. Denounces French occupation of Ruhr and calls on Britain and America to intervene.
1924	54	Smuts loses election to Nationalists and Labour. Heads the opposition.
1926	56	Smuts publishes *Holism and Evolution*. Balfour Declaration recognises autonomy of Dominions.
1930	60	Smuts made a Fellow of the Royal Society. Tours America.
1931	61	Smuts becomes President of British Association for the Advancement of Science. Statute of Westminster confirms autonomy of Dominions.
1933	63	After severe economic depression, South Africa goes off gold standard. Smuts and Hertzog merge their parties to form the United Party. Smuts serves under Hertzog as Deputy Prime Minister.

YEAR	HISTORY	CULTURE
1923	French and Belgian troops occupy the Ruhr when Germany fails to make reparation payments.	P G Wodehouse, *The Inimitable Jeeves.* George Gershwin, *Rhapsody in Blue.*
1924	Labour Party loses general election after *Daily Mail* publishes Zinoviev Letter.	King George V makes first royal radio broadcast, opening British Empire Exhibition at Wembley.
1926	General Strike in Britain. Germany admitted to League of Nations.	A A Milne, *Winnie the Pooh.* Ernest Hemingway, *The Sun Also Rises.*
1930	British Imperial Conference held in London: Statute of Westminster approved.	W H Auden, *Poems.* Film: *All Quiet on the Western Front.*
1931	National Government formed in Britain. Britain abandons Gold Standard.	William Faulkner, *Sanctuary.* Film: *Little Caesar.*
1933	Adolf Hitler appointed Chancellor of Germany. Japan announces it will leave League of Nations. Germany withdraws from League of Nations and Disarmament Conference.	George Orwell, *Down and Out in Paris and London.* Duke Ellington's Orchestra debuts in Britain. Film: *Queen Christina.*

YEAR	AGE	THE LIFE AND THE LAND
1934	64	Smuts in England recommends *complete equality of status* as cure for Germany's *inferiority complex.*
1936	66	Hertzog amends constitution to restrict black franchise in Cape Province.
1938	68	Afrikaner nationalist movement, *Ossewa Brandwag*, founded. Munich Crisis. Smuts assents to Hertzog's declaration of South African neutrality.
1939	69	As Minister of Justice, Smuts sends police into South-West Africa to forestall pro-Nazi coup. Smuts becomes Prime Minister, Foreign Minister and Minister of Defence. South Africa declares war on Germany.
1941	71	Allied defeat at Tobruk. 25,000 South Africans taken prisoner.

YEAR	HISTORY	CULTURE
1934	Germany: 'Night of the Long Knives'; role of German President and Chancellor merged, Hitler becomes *Führer*. USSR admitted to League of Nations.	Robert Graves, *I, Claudius*. Dmitri Shostakovich, *Lady Macbeth of Mtsensk*. Film: *David Copperfield*.
1936	German troops occupy Rhineland violating Treaty of Versailles.	Aldous Huxley, *Eyeless in Gaza*. Berlin Olympics. Film: *Modern Times*.
1938	German troops enter Austria declaring it part of German Reich. Munich Agreement hands Sudetenland to Germany.	Graham Greene, *Brighton Rock*. Film: *Alexander Nevsky*.
1939	German troops enter Prague. Germany demands Danzig and Polish Corridor: Poland refuses. Nazi-Soviet Pact agrees no fighting, partition of Poland. Second World War begins.	Bela Bartok, *String Quartet No. 6*. James Joyce, *Finnegan's Wake*. Thomas Mann, *Lotte in Weimar*. John Steinbeck, *The Grapes of Wrath*. Film: *Gone with the Wind*.
1941	Second World War: Germany invades USSR. Japan attacks Pearl Harbor; Germany and Italy declare war on US.	Noel Coward, *Blithe Spirit*. Film: *Citizen Kane*.

YEAR	AGE	THE LIFE AND THE LAND
1942	72	South Africans take part in Allied landings in Madagascar. Smuts in Cairo urges change of command in North Africa campaign. South Africans take part in victory of El Alamein.
1944	74	Smuts accompanies Churchill to France after D-Day landings.
1945	75	Smuts at San Francisco for founding of United Nations. Drafts Preamble to UN Charter. Confirms policy of white supremacy in South Africa.
1946	76	Jul–Oct: Smuts in Paris to represent South Africa at Peace Conference.
		Dec: Smuts appears before United Nations to argue for incorporation of South-West Africa in South Africa. His plea rejected.
1947	77	Smuts receives British royal family in South Africa.

YEAR	HISTORY	CULTURE
1942	Second World War: Singapore surrenders to Japanese: Japanese invade Burma. Battle of Stalingrad in USSR. Eisenhower lands in Morocco and Algeria.	Enid Blyton publishes first 'Famous Five' book, *Five on a Treasure Island*. Jean Anouilh, *Antigone*. Film: *Casablanca*.
1944	British and US forces in Italy liberate Rome. Free French enter Paris.	Terrence Rattigan, *The Winslow Boy*. Tennessee Williams, *The Glass Menagerie*. Film: *Henry V*.
1945	Second World War: Hitler commits suicide in Berlin; city surrenders to Soviets. VE Day: 8 May. US drops atomic bombs on Hiroshima and Nagasaki: Japan surrenders to Allies.	Benjamin Britten, *Peter Grimes*. George Orwell, *Animal Farm*. Film: *Brief Encounter*.
1946	UN General Assembly opens in London. Churchill declares Stalin has lowered 'Iron Curtain' across Europe, signalling formal start of Cold War. Greek Civil War begins.	Bertrand Russell, *History of Western Philosophy*. Film: *Great Expectations*. Radio: Alistair Cook's *Letter from America* begins (series ends in 2004).
1947	'Truman Doctrine' pledges to support 'free peoples resisting subjugation by armed minorities or outside pressures'.	Anne Frank, *The Diary of Anne Frank*. Film: *Monsieur Verdoux*.

YEAR	AGE	THE LIFE AND THE LAND
1948	78	May: Smuts among first to recognise State of Israel. Loses general election to Malan. Apartheid institutionalised in South Africa.
		Jun: Smuts installed as Chancellor of Cambridge University.
		Oct: Smut's son, Japie, dies suddenly.
1950	80	May: Smuts celebrates his 80th birthday but suffers a heart attack.
		September: Smuts dies at Doornkloof.

YEAR	HISTORY	CULTURE
1948	Burmese independence. Gandhi assassinated in India: last British troops leave. Western Allies organise Berlin Airlift after USSR blockades Berlin.	Graham Greene, *The Heart of the Matter*. London Olympics. Film: *Whisky Galore*.
1950	Korean War breaks out. West Germany joins Council of Europe.	Ezra Pound, *Seventy Cantos*. Film: *Sunset Boulevard*.

Further Reading

For a survey of older biographies, see Piet Beukes, *The Holistic Smuts. A study in personality* (Human and Rousseau, Cape Town: 1989) pp 18–25. The monumental standard biography by W K Hancock is in two volumes: *Smuts 1: The Sanguine Years 1870–1919* (Cambridge University Press, London: 1962) and *Smuts 2: The Fields of Force 1919–1950* (Cambridge University Press, London: 1968). Sarah Millin's *General Smuts,* in two volumes (Faber and Faber, London: 1936); her *The Measure of My Days* (Faber and Faber, London: 1955) and, despite occasional inaccuracies, J C Smuts's life of his father, *Jan Christian Smuts* (Cassel, London: 1952) all have the advantage of personal knowledge. Other useful first-hand accounts are Piet Beukes, *The Religious Smuts* (Human and Rousseau, Cape Town: 1994) and Kathleen Mincher, *I Lived in His Shadow. My Life with General Smuts* (Bailey Bros. and Swinfen, London: 1965). Two other valuable studies by Beukes are *The Holistic Smuts. A Study in Personality* (Human and Rousseau, Cape Town: 1989) and *The Romantic Smuts. Women and Love in his Life* (Human and Rousseau: Cape Town, 1992). Deneys Reitz, *Commando. A Boer Journal of the Boer War* (Faber & Faber, London: 1929, latest reprint 2005) is a classic account. There is some fascinating film footage of Smuts on British Pathé news clips (available on the internet) and recordings of his broadcasts at the British Library Sound Archive.

The historian of Smuts at the Peace Conference has a wealth of published primary sources in Smuts's fascinating and moving correspondence for 1919 in Volume IV of *Selections from the Smuts Papers*, edited by W K Hancock and Jean Van der Poel (Cambridge University Press, London: 1966). Smuts at the Conference features in A Lentin, *Lloyd George, Woodrow Wilson and the Guilt of Germany: An essay in the pre-history of Appeasement* (Leicester University Press, Bath: 1984), republished as *Guilt at Versailles. Lloyd George and the Pre-History of Appeasement* (Methuen, London: 1985), and more especially in his *Lloyd George and the Lost Peace: from Versailles to Hitler, 1919–1940* (Palgrave, Basingstoke: 2001) pp 67–88. Smuts's controversial memorandum on pensions is discussed in A Lentin, 'Maynard Keynes and the "Bamboozlement" of Woodrow Wilson: What Really Happened at Paris? (Wilson, Lloyd George, pensions and pre-armistice agreement)' *Diplomacy & Statecraft,* 15 (4) (2004) pp 725–63.

The best short account of the Peace Conference and Peace Treaties is Alan Sharp, *The Versailles Settlement: Peacemaking in Paris, 1919* (2nd edition, Macmillan, Basingstoke: 2008). Jacques Bainville, *Les conséquences politiques de la paix* (éditions de l'arsenal, Paris: 1995), first published in 1919, remains a prophetic masterpiece of analysis and perception. Harold Nicolson, *Peacemaking 1919* (Constable, London: 1933, reprinted 1964, 2001), is still in my opinion the classic account. For a robust defence of peacemakers and Treaty, see William R Keylor, 'Versailles and International Diplomacy,' in *The Treaty of Versailles. A Reassessment after 75 Years,*

Manfred F Boemeke, Gerald D Feldman and Elisabeth Glaser
(ed) (Cambridge University Press, London: 1998) pp 469–505.

Bibliography
Archive Sources
Robert Cecil, Diary, British Library
Herbert Fisher Papers, Bodleian Library, Oxford
Foreign Office Papers, The National Archives
Hankey Papers, Churchill College, Cambridge
Lloyd George Papers, House of Lords Record Office
Smuts Papers, Cambridge University Library
Smuts, 'Our policy at the Peace Conference', 3 December
    1918, National Archives FO 311/3451

Primary Printed Sources
C Addison, *Politics from Within 1911–1918* (Herbert
    Jenkins, London: 1924)
L S Amery, *My Political Life,* Vol. 2, *War and Peace 1914–
    1929* (Hutchinson, London: 1953)
P B Blankenberg, *The Thoughts of General Smuts.
    Compiled by his Private Secretary* (Juta and Co, Cape
    Town: 1951)
*British Documents on Foreign Affairs. Reports and Papers
    from the Foreign Office Confidential Prints,* K Bourne
    and D C Watt (ed), Part 2, Series 1, *The Paris Peace
    Conference of 1919,* M Dockrill (ed), Vol. 4, *British
    Empire Delegation Minutes* (University Publications of
    America, Bethesda MD: 1989)
*Foreign Relations of the United States. The Paris Peace
    Conference, 1919,* Vol. 5 (United States Department of
    State, Washington DC: 1946)

D Hart-Davis (ed), *King's Counsellor. Abdication and War: The Diaries of Sir Alan Lascelles* (Weidenfeld and Nicolson, London: 2006)

W K Hancock and J Van der Poel (eds), *Selections from the Smuts Papers* 7 Volumes (Cambridge University Press, Cambridge: 1966–1973)

A S Link (ed), *The Papers of Woodrow Wilson,* Vols 54–67 (Princeton University Press, Princeton N J: 1986–1992)

J McEwen (ed), *The Riddell Diaries 1908–1923* (Athlone Press, London: 1986)

P Mantoux, *Les Délibérations du Conseil des Quatre: Notes de l'officier interprète,* Vol. 1 (Centre National de la Recherche Scientifique, Paris: 1955)

K Middlemas (ed), T Jones, *Whitehall Diary,* Vol. 1 (Oxford University Press, Oxford: 1969)

N Nicolson (ed), H. Nicolson, *Diaries and Letters 1939–1945* (Collins, London: 1967)

N Nicolson (ed), H. Nicolson, *Diaries and Letters 1945–62* (Collins, London: 1969)

Lord Riddell, *Intimate Diary of the Peace Conference and After* (Gollancz, London: 1933)

C Seymour (ed), *The Intimate Papers of Colonel House,* Vol. 3 (Houghton Mifflin, Boston, MA: 1928)

J C Smuts, *The League of Nations: a Practical Suggestion* (Hodder and Stoughton, London: 1918)

J C Smuts, *Memoirs of the Boer War,* Gail Nattrass and S.B. Spiess (ed) (Jonathan Bull Publishers, Johannesburg: 1994)

J C Smuts, Speech to both Houses of Parliament, 21 October 1942, *Journal of the Royal African Society,* Vol. 42 (167) April 1943, pp 59–68

J C Smuts, Speech to Royal Institute of International
Affairs, 13 November 1934, *International Affairs,* Vol. 14
(1) Jan-Feb 1935, pp 3–19.

J C Smuts, *War-Time Speeches* (Hodder and Stoughton,
London: 1917)

Frances Stevenson, *Lloyd George. A Diary* (Hutchinson,
London: 1971)

T Wilson (ed), *The Political Diaries of C P Scott 1911–1928*
(Collins, London: 1970)

The New York Times

The Times

Secondary Sources

J Bainville, *Les conséquences politiques de la paix, 1919*
(éditions de l'Arsenal, Paris: 1995)

Lord Beaverbrook, *Men and Power 1917–1918* (Hutchinson,
London: 1956)

P Beukes, *The Religious Smuts* (Human and Rousseau, Cape
Town: 1994)

P Beukes, *The Romantic Smuts. Women and Love in his Life*
(Human and Rousseau, Cape Town: 1992)

P Beukes, *The Holistic Smuts. A Study in Personality*
(Human and Rousseau, Cape Town: 1989)

M Boemeke, G Feldman and Elisabeth Glaser (eds), *The
Treaty of Versailles. A Reassessment after 75 Years*
(Cambridge University Press, Cambridge: 1998)

R E Bunselmeyer, *The Costs of the War 1914–1919* (Archon
Books, Hamden, CT: 1975)

C E Callwell, *Field-Marshal Sir Henry Wilson, His Life and
Diaries,* Vol. 2 (Cassell, London: 1927)

G Dangerfield, *The Damnable Question. A Study in Anglo-
Irish Relations* (Quartet Books, London: 1979)

T R H Davenport, *South Africa. A Modern History* (MacMillan, London: 1978)

M Dockrill and J Fisher (eds), *The Paris Peace Conference, 1919. Peace without Victory?* (Polgrave in association with the Public Record Office, Basingstoke: 2001)

L F Fitzhardinge, *The Little Digger 1914–1952. William Morris Hughes. A Political Biography,* Vol. 2 (Angus and Robertson, Sydney: 1979)

Zelda Friedlander (ed), *Jan Smuts Remembered: A Centennial Tribute* (Allan Wingate, London: 1970)

M G Fry, 'Agents and Structures: The Dominions and the Czechoslovak Crisis, September 1938' in I Lukes and E Goldstein, *The Munich Crisis, 1938. Prelude to World War II* (Frank Cass, London: 1999) pp 293–341

M Fry, 'British Revisionism', in Boemeke, Feldman and Glaser, pp 565–601

E Goldstein, *Winning the Peace. British Diplomatic Strategy, Peace Planning, and the Paris Peace Conference 1916–1920* (Oxford University Press, Oxford: 1991)

J Grigg, *Lloyd George. War Leader 1916–1918* (Allen Lane, London: 2002)

T J Haarhof, *Smuts the Humanist: a Personal Reminiscence* (Blackwell, Oxford: 1970)

W K Hancock, *Smuts,* Vol. 1, *The Sanguine Years 1870–1919* (Cambridge University Press, Cambridge: 1962)

W K Hancock, *Smuts,* Vol. 2, *The Fields of Force 1919–1950* (Cambridge University Press, Cambridge: 1968)

H Harmer, *Friedrich Ebert* (Haus Publishing, London: 2008)

D Heater, *National Self-Determination. Woodrow Wilson and his Legacy* (St Martin's Press, London: 1994)

R Hyam, 'Souith Africa, Cambridge, and Commonwealth History', *The Round Table* (2001), Vol. 90 (360) pp 401–14

R Jenkins, *Churchill* (Pan Books, London: 2002)

K A Keppel-Jones, *South Africa. A Short History,* 5th Edition (Hutchinson, London: 1982)

W R Keylor, 'Versailles and International Diplomacy', in Boemeke, Feldman and Glaser, pp 469–505

J M Keynes, *The Economic Consequences of the Peace* (Labour Research Department, Westminster: 1920 edition)

Alma Luckau, *The German Delegation at the Paris Peace Conference* (Columbia University Press, New York: 1940)

A Lentin, 'Maynard Keynes and the "Bamboozlement" of Woodrow Wilson: What Really Happened at Paris? (Wilson, Lloyd George, Pensions and Pre-Armistice Agreement', *Diplomacy & Statecraft,* 15 (4), 2004, pp 725–63

A Lentin, *Guilt at Versailles. Lloyd George and the Pre-History of Appeasement* (Methuen, London: 1984, 1985)

A Lentin, *Lloyd George and the Lost Peace. From Versailles to Hitler, 1919–1940* (Palgrave, London: 2001)

D Lloyd George, *War Memoirs,* Vols 1–2 (Odham, London: 1938)

D Lloyd George, *Memoirs of the Peace Conference,* Vols 1–2 (Yale University Press, New Haven, CT: 1939)

M Lojko, 'Mission Impossible: General Smuts, Sir George Clerk and British Diplomacy in Central Europe in 1919', in Dockrill and Fisher, pp 115–39

W R Louis, *Great Britain and Germany's Lost Colonies 1914–1919* (Oxford University Press, Oxford: 1967)

N Mandela, *Long Walk to Freedom. The Autobiography of Nelson Mandela* (Little Brown and Co, New York: 1994)

C A W Manning, ' "Empire" into "Commonwealth" ', in G A Panichas (ed), *Promise of Greatness. The War of 1914–1918* (Cassell, London: 1968) pp 426–37

G Martel, 'O What an Ugly Peace' (review of M Boemeke, G Feldman and Elisabeth Glaser). H-Diplo. Roundtable, 2 March 2001.

Sarah Millin, *General Smuts,* Vols 1–2 (Faber and Faber, London: 1936)

Sarah Millin, *The People of South Africa* (Constable, London: 1951)

Sarah Millin, *The Measure of My Days* (Faber and Faber, London: 1955)

Lord Moran, *Winston Churchill. The Struggle for Survival 1940–65* (Constable, London: 1966)

H Nicolson, *Peacemaking 1919* (Constable, London: 1933)

F Owen, *Tempestuous Journey. Lloyd George, His Life and Times* (Hutchinson, London: 1954)

D Reitz, *Commando. A Boer Journal of the Boer War* (Faber and Faber, London: 1929, 1935 edition)

Salute to a Great South African. Jan Christian Smuts (Cape Times Ltd, Cape Town: 1950)

Lord Shaw of Dunfermline, *Letters to Isabel* (George H Doran Co, New York: 1921)

J C Smuts, *Jan Christian Smuts* (Cassell, London: 1952)

Mary Soames, *Clementine Churchill* (Cassell, London: 1979)

A Toynbee, *Acquaintances* (Oxford University Press, Oxford: 1967)

Freda Troup, *South Africa. An Historical Introduction* (Eyre Methuen, London: 1972)

P Van der Byl, *Top Hat to Velskoen* (Timmins, Cape Town: 1973)

S D Waley, *Edwin Montagu: A Memoir and an account of his visits to India* (Asia Publishing House, London: 1964)

A Walworth, *Wilson and his Peacemakers. American Diplomacy at the Paris Peace Conference, 1919* (Norton, New York: 1986)

C Weizmann, *Trial and Error* (Hamish Hamilton, London: 1949)

P J Yearwood, *Guarantee of Peace. The League of Nations in British Policy 1914–1925* (Oxford University Press, Oxford: 2009)

Zara Steiner, 'The Treaty of Versailles Revisited', in Dockrill and Fisher, pp 13–33

Picture Sources

The author and publishers wish to express their thanks to the following sources of illustrative material and/or permission to reproduce it. They will make proper acknowledgements in future editions in the event that any omissions have occurred.

Illustrations courtesy of Topham Picturepoint and Getty Images.

Endpapers
The Signing of Peace in the Hall of Mirrors, Versailles, 28th June 1919 by Sir William Orpen (Imperial War Museum: Bridgeman Art Library)
Front row: Dr Johannes Bell (Germany) signing with Herr Hermann Müller leaning over him
Middle row (seated, left to right): General Tasker H Bliss, Col E M House, Mr Henry White, Mr Robert Lansing, President Woodrow Wilson (United States); M Georges Clemenceau (France); Mr David Lloyd George, Mr Andrew Bonar Law, Mr Arthur J Balfour, Viscount Milner, Mr G N Barnes (Great Britain); Prince Saionji (Japan)

Back row (left to right): M Eleftherios Venizelos (Greece);
Dr Afonso Costa (Portugal); Lord Riddell (British Press);
Sir George E Foster (Canada); M Nikola Pašić (Serbia);
M Stephen Pichon (France); Col Sir Maurice Hankey,
Mr Edwin S Montagu (Great Britain); the Maharajah of
Bikaner (India); Signor Vittorio Emanuele Orlando (Italy);
M Paul Hymans (Belgium); General Louis Botha (South
Africa); Mr W M Hughes (Australia)

Jacket images

(Front): Imperial War Museum: akg Images.
(Back): *Peace Conference at the Quai d'Orsay* by Sir William
Orpen (Imperial War Museum: akg Images).
Left to right (seated): Signor Orlando (Italy); Mr Robert
Lansing, President Woodrow Wilson (United States); M
Georges Clemenceau (France); Mr David Lloyd George, Mr
Andrew Bonar Law, Mr Arthur J Balfour (Great Britain);
Left to right (standing): M Paul Hymans (Belgium); Mr
Eleftherios Venizelos (Greece); The Emir Feisal (The
Hashemite Kingdom); Mr W F Massey (New Zealand);
General Jan Smuts (South Africa); Col E M House (United
States); General Louis Botha (South Africa); Prince Saionji
(Japan); Mr W M Hughes (Australia); Sir Robert Borden
(Canada); Mr G N Barnes (Great Britain); M Ignacy
Paderewski (Poland)

Index

Brockdorff-Rantzau, Count
   Ulrich von 83
Broederbond
   (Brotherhood), the 135

C

Campbell-Bannerman, Sir
   Henry 16, 17, 21
Canada 56
Cecil, Lord Robert 53,
   58–9, 88, 89, 97, 104,
   125
Chamberlain, Austen 37,
   97, 99–100
Chamberlain, Joseph 9, 10
Churchill, Winston 34–5,
   45, 97, 99, 131, 148,
   152–3
   and Smuts in the Second
      World War 138–41,
      144
Clark, Alice 20, 38, 50, 59,
   64, 74, 75, 81, 83, 93, 95,
   108–9, 110, 117, 122, 125
Clark, Hilda 64, 91
Clark, Margaret *see*
   Margaret Gillett
Clemenceau, Georges 57,
   64, 69–70, 71, 79, 82, 90,
   96, 104, 118, 121, 152
Czechoslovakia 54, 68, 73,
   102, 107, 132

D

Danzig 66, 68, 70, 81, 93,
   107, 132–3, 134
De Valera, Eamon 126
Diaz, Bartholomew 3
Dulles, John Foster 78

E

Edward VII, King 23

F

First World War, the 30–45
Fisher, Herbert 97–8, 103
Foster, Sir George 100, 101
Fourie, Major Jopie 31,
   136
Fourteen Points, the 41, 60,
   67–8, 95–7, 99–102, 107,
   118
France 3, 40, 49, 51, 62, 65,
   66, 76, 82, 84–5, 89, 93–5,
   108, 121, 125–7, 130, 138,
   139, 140, 143, 145

G

Gandhi, Mohandas 29
George V, King 37, 126
George VI, King 140, 145
German East Africa 32–3,
   34, 40, 60
German South-West Africa
   13, 31, 32, 39–40, 59,

Makers of the Modern World

UK PUBLICATION: November 2008 to December 2010
CLASSIFICATION: Biography/History/
   International Relations
FORMAT: 198 × 128mm
EXTENT: 208pp
ILLUSTRATIONS: 6 photographs plus 4 maps
TERRITORY: world

Chronology of life in context, full index, bibliography innovative layout
with sidebars